PRAISE FC

M0002099975

"Helping people to authentically display leadership presence. I love what Carol Kinsey Goman does!"
Michael Massari, Chief Sales Officer, Caesars Entertainment

"Internalize the clear-headed wisdom and proven expertise provided by Carol Kinsey Goman in her best book yet and move forward with enhanced self-awareness. If you want to take your career to the next level and higher, get this book!"
Leslie J. Saleson, Founder and CEO, Hi Rise Network

"This book reinforces many of the key tenets I have learned about the importance of leadership presence from one of the world's premier leadership institutes, the U.S. Army. The six Cs: Credibility, Confidence, Composure, Connection, Charisma, and Cross-cultural leadership will assist everyone in enhancing their leadership presence, self-awareness, and overall effectiveness."
Josh Woody, Captain, U.S. Army

"Carol Kinsey Goman is an expert on the impact of body language on leadership presence. This is a must-read!"
Cheryl Berrington, Principal, Berrington Group

"With her keen eye for detail and a knack for taking complex non-verbal research findings and translating them into actionable skills, Carol Kinsey Goman stands out in communicating how to create and maintain authentic leadership presence in the workplace. Goman authoritatively,

yet engagingly, informs the reader how to project presence across multiple contexts and situations."
Patrick A. Stewart, PhD, Associate Professor of Political Science, University of Arkansas, Fayetteville, and author of *Debatable Humor: Laughing Matters on the 2008 Presidential Primary Campaign*

"The time for women leadership has come. Women have made impressive gains in politics and the business world, making their voices heard and breaking the glass ceiling of organizations and boardrooms. Carol Kinsey Goman is an expert on the impact of body language on leadership presence. *Stand Out* should be on the reading list for every woman leader."
Barbara Dietrich, CEO, Diplomatic World (Belgium)

"The groundwater of customer loyalty is trust, expressed as authenticity. It is also the feature that makes leaders trusted. Carol's profound book reveals ways leaders can source and express this powerful feature they already possess."
Chip R. Bell, bestselling author of *Inside Your Customer's Imagination: 5 Secrets for Creating Breakthrough Products, Services, and Solutions*

"Carol Kinsey Goman is always one of the most talked about speakers at our London events. The authenticity and clarity with which she discusses body language and leadership presence inspires and keeps the audience's attention. You'll find this book is likewise both attention-grabbing and inspiring."
Afi Ofori, Managing Director, Zars Media (UK)

"Confident, credible, and empathetic. Three words existing and aspiring leaders need to heed to stand out. Yet again, Carol Kinsey Goman's lucid insights illustrate the true power of presence."
Rob Briggs, Director, Graystone Communications, and author of 'Organizational Trust' in the *IABC Global Handbook* (UK)

"To be the most influential, women need to build on the unique talents and strengths we bring to our organizations. That takes leadership presence—and this valuable book gives insights into how others perceive us, and how to project our best authentic selves."
Yanina Dubeykovskaya, Founder, Women Influence Community (Russia)

"Carol Kinsey Goman consistently wows our audiences with her rare insights about what it takes to be a confident and authentic leader, and how to use those traits to inspire others. This book is filled with her insights."
Christina Corrigan, Deputy Executive Director, Communications/Programs, Texas Municipal League

"Never has there been a greater need to stand out above the din and disruptions thrown at us all. In *Stand Out*, Carol Kinsey Goman shows you exactly how to lead others when their attention is short, their hearts crave connection, and their passions are seeking you—the leader they need during these chaotic times."
Bill Jensen, bestselling author of *Disrupt!* and *Future Strong*

"Carol Kinsey Goman knows better what is needed in leadership. It's not just about being eloquent, it's about knowing how to act. In other words, you need to know what the other person is looking for. When it comes to projecting leadership, you'll get a lot out of this book."
Kaz Amemiya, President, Crossmedia Communications, Inc. (Japan)

"Carol Kinsey Goman shows you the importance and impact of presence to be an inspiring and authentic leader."
Michael Rudnick, CEO, Velaku Software

"With a deep experience in leading global fashion and beauty businesses, I am often asked: How did you get to the top? How did you succeed in a mostly male-dominated corporate environment? How did you build a network? While there are no cookie-cutter answers, Carol Kinsey Goman provides a practical, accessible, real-life guide to unleashing your full potential as a leader."
Laure de Metz, General Manager, BITE Beauty

"Carol Kinsey Goman is right—a title alone doesn't give you presence. I've watched celebrities and successful executives project their own special brand of charisma to land them roles and sell ideas. In the end, your presence is the most valuable resource you have."
Garrett DeLorm, Executive Producer, Camp+King

"A title is what someone gives you as a result of your expertise and hard work. But leadership is more than a title; it's an attitude, a presence. In order to become highly effective and memorable, you have to cultivate traits that align with who you are and the image you want to portray. Carol Kinsey Goman's book offers actionable steps that ensure you stand out and leave a lasting impression. Pick up the book, put those steps to practice, and become the leader that others want to follow."
Jeffrey Hayzlett, primetime TV and podcast host, speaker, author, and part-time cowboy

Stand Out

How to Build Your
Leadership Presence

Carol Kinsey Goman

KoganPage

Publisher's note

Every possible effort has been made to ensure that the information contained in this book is accurate at the time of going to press, and the publishers and authors cannot accept responsibility for any errors or omissions, however caused. No responsibility for loss or damage occasioned to any person acting, or refraining from action, as a result of the material in this publication can be accepted by the editor, the publisher or the author.

First published in Great Britain and the United States in 2021 by Kogan Page Limited

2nd Floor, 45 Gee Street	122 W 27th Street, 10th Floor	4737/23 Ansari Road
London	New York, NY 10001	Daryaganj
EC1V 3RS	USA	New Delhi 110002
United Kingdom		India

www.koganpage.com

Kogan Page books are printed on paper from sustainable forests.

ISBNs

Hardback	978 1 78966 583 3
Paperback	978 1 78966 581 9
Ebook	978 1 78966 582 6

Library of Congress Control Number

2020941951

British Library Cataloguing-in-Publication Data

A CIP record for this book is available from the British Library.

Typeset by Hong Kong FIVE Workshop
Print production managed by Jellyfish
Printed and bound by CPI Group (UK) Ltd, Croydon CR0 4YY

CONTENTS

ABOUT THE AUTHOR

Carol Kinsey Goman, PhD (https://CarolKinseyGoman.com) is an international keynote speaker and seminar leader for corporations, conventions, universities, and government agencies. Carol's clients include over 400 organizations in 28 countries—corporate giants such as Consolidated Edison, 3M, and PepsiCo; major nonprofit organizations such as the American Institute of Banking, the Healthcare Forum, and the American Society of Training and Development; high-tech firms such as Hewlett-Packard and Texas Instruments; agencies such as the Office of the Comptroller of the Currency, Lawrence Livermore Laboratory, and the Library of Congress; and international organizations such as Kuwait Oil, Dairy Farm in Hong Kong, Petrofac in the UAE, SCA Hygiene in Germany, BNP Paribas in England, and European Women in Technology in the Netherlands.

Carol is a leadership contributor for Forbes.com, the author of 12 other business books, including *The Silent Language of Leaders: How Body Language Can Help—or Hurt—How You Lead*, and the creator of two video training courses for LinkedIn Learning: "Body Language for Leaders" and "Collaborative Leadership".

She is a faculty member for the Institute for Management Studies, offering seminars throughout the United States, and for Excellence Squared Academy, offering programs in Canada and Europe. She has also served as adjunct faculty at John F. Kennedy University in the International MBA program, at the University of California in the Executive Education Department, and for the Chamber of Commerce of the United States at their Institutes for Organization Management.

As an executive coach, Carol has two specialties: assisting leaders and entrepreneurs as they craft and deliver key messages and helping managers prepare for senior positions by increasing their leadership presence, which she defines as "the ability to influence and impact others by projecting confidence, credibility, composure, connection, and charisma."

Introduction

I was recently asked to coach a candidate for a senior-level leadership position in a Silicon Valley technology firm. I learned that this man's work was of the highest caliber and that his advancement had been fast-tracked—until now.

When I asked the president of the company why this talented man's career had suddenly stalled, I was told that he didn't have the leadership presence needed to advance higher in the organization. My coaching assignment was to help him communicate with increased credibility, confidence, composure, connection, and charisma.

Notice that my job wasn't to help him *develop* those qualities but rather to help him *display* them. The ability to do so is, in a nutshell, the essence of projecting leadership presence.

I'm an international speaker, the author of 13 business books, and a leadership presence coach for managers, team leaders, entrepreneurs, and senior executives who are looking for ways to become even more effective in their ability to impact and influence others.

I wrote this book for you and the other high performers I haven't had the opportunity to coach personally. I want to help you stand out as the talented leader you already are.

As a leadership contributor for Forbes.com, each year I receive dozens of books to review. I scan each one to find the actionable tips that I can pass on to my readers. You won't have to scan to find tips in this book. *Stand Out* is filled with tips, strategies, and action steps that you can apply immediately for positive results. Here is a brief overview:

Chapter 1, "Leadership Presence," begins with the definition of "leadership presence" as "a blend of attitudes, qualities, and behaviors that makes you stand out and gives your career that extra boost." But leadership presence isn't automatically assigned to you because of your title or expertise. Instead, leadership presence is what people say about you after you leave the room. It's all about the perception people have after interacting with you of how well you display credibility, confidence, composure, connection, and charisma. This is why impression management is the key, and aligning people's impression of you with your best authentic self is the goal.

Chapter 2, "Credibility," covers the communication skills leaders need to be perceived as competent and believable. You'll find tips for structuring your comments in ways that underscore your expertise. You'll learn how to monitor signs of engagement and disengagement so that you can judge how your comments are being received and get tips on how to respond if you lose people's attention. Although face-to-face communication gives you the best opportunity to impact and influence others, I'll also show you how to increase your credibility in an email, a telephone conversation, and a videoconference.

Chapter 3, "Confidence," focuses on the trait most commonly associated with displaying leadership presence and the one that's almost impossible to fake. In this chapter, you'll learn how to overcome the obstacles to building a positive self-image and how to tap into your authentic confidence, even if you are feeling unsure. Since confidence is being evaluated every time you speak, your communication style and word choices are highly influential. I'll show you which words makes you appear less confident than you really are and give you tips for displaying your confident best whether you are participating in a meeting or giving a formal presentation.

Chapter 4, "Composure," helps you stay poised under pressure by creating the habits that keep stress at a positive, healthy, and energizing level. You'll learn strategies for interrupting the trigger-response reaction, understand when and why you should say "no," and gain tips for keeping cool while handling interruptions, answering tough questions, responding to challenges, and dealing with a bully.

Chapter 5, "Connection," provides an overview of ways to empathetically connect and inspire those with whom you work. In this chapter, we'll look at the powerful impact of emotional intelligence on your ability to display leadership presence through actions that include empathetic listening, creating psychological safety, and showing social sensitivity. You'll learn the five quickest ways to connect with someone and why connection is needed more than ever to address what is currently being called a loneliness epidemic.

Chapter 6, "Charisma," is about how you can exude charisma without necessarily being flamboyant, extroverted, or commanding. In fact, for business leaders, charisma is less a quality in itself as it is a style of leadership presence based in your special character and talents. Whether your style of charisma is based on confidence, credibility, composure, or connection, you'll discover that your innate charismatic qualities are best revealed when you play to your strengths.

Chapter 7, "Body Language for Leadership Presence," covers the impact of nonverbal communication on leadership presence. When I started to coach organizational leaders, I saw that most were nonverbally illiterate—completely out of touch with the effect their body language had on others and unaware of the clear signals that were being sent by clients and colleagues in every business encounter. But that won't be you! In this chapter, you'll learn the two sets of nonverbal signals that people look for in all leaders, how to make a positive first impression in the first few seconds of meeting someone, how to use body language to highlight your verbal messages, and how to read the nonverbal signals that indicate bluffing or deception.

One of the most career-limiting comments I've heard was from a senior executive in human resources when a highly qualified candidate didn't get a promotion. The reason provided was "The evaluation committee had no idea who she was."

Chapter 8, "Self-Promotion," gives you guidelines for increasing your visibility so that people know how talented you are. You'll get tips for personal branding, preparing your elevator speech, using social media, finding mentors and sponsors, and sharpening your networking skills.

Chapter 9, "Leadership Presence for Women," offers insights into the strengths and attributes that women bring to the organization. It looks at the unique challenges women face when it comes to being perceived as leaders and offers proven strategies for overcoming those challenges, including how to bridge the confidence gap, develop conscious competence, and stop waiting to be perfect. You'll learn the body language traps that women fall into and tips to avoid them. You'll get a list of dos and don'ts about what it means to dress for success and why I advise women leaders to bring their femininity to work.

Chapter 10, "Cross-Cultural Leadership Presence," compares and contrasts leadership presence in different cultures. If you work internationally or lead a global team, this chapter will show you how, from culture to culture, the norms differ in regard to the amount of eye contact you should make, whether you should be direct or talk around an issue, and if being reserved or enthusiastic gives you leadership presence. You'll learn the cross-cultural communication skills a leader needs to display to be seen as confident, credible, and empathetic, and the universal qualities that we look for in all leaders.

The Conclusion, "Leading in Times of Uncertainty and Change," reflects the challenges and opportunities that leaders in today's organizations are facing.

One final note: Throughout this book, you'll see graphics that visually reinforce my key points. I would like to acknowledge the work of Brian O'Mara-Croft, of Visual Congruence, who created all these graphics and is my go-to resource for all PowerPoint slides and media materials.

I would also like to thank Kathe Sweeney of Kogan Page for the time, energy, and talent she put into editing and (most of all) for her unwavering support.

Last, a huge thank you to my husband, Ray K. Goman, who had to live with me through the writing process.

1

Leadership Presence

"She's warm and personable, but she doesn't have the gravitas we are looking for in an executive."

"It isn't that he couldn't do the job. It's that no one else sees him in that role."

"She looks too fragile to be a strong leader."

"He's got all the qualifications, but he's such a poor communicator that no one listens when he speaks."

These are the kinds of comments I hear about the talented people I coach. My clients know every detail of their business or job function, contribute substantially to the success of their organizations, and are highly competent professionals in practically every way, and yet . . . something is missing. *Leadership presence.*

Leadership presence is that elusive "we know it when we see it" factor that turns good managers into outstanding leaders who are rewarded with recognition and advancement. It is a blend of attitudes, qualities, and behaviors that makes you stand out from your peers and gives your career that extra boost. It's evaluated by how actively you engage and contribute in meetings, how credible and confident you come across when speaking, how poised you are under pressure, and how skilled you are at influencing others in ways that are authentic, empathetic, and motivational.

Now that you know what leadership presence is, it's important to clarify what it is not:

- It's not an attribute that is automatically assigned to you because of your title, technical expertise, or business acumen.
- It's not necessarily reflective of your true leadership qualities or potential.[1]

And don't assume that your leadership presence is evidenced by what people say directly to you. It's often more about what they say after you've left the room.

Looking like a leader, being perceived as a leader, when you interact with customers, peers, and executives is the essence of leadership presence.[2]

Leadership Presence Is Impression Management

Leadership presence is all about impression management. As such, it requires a deep understanding of the impact of your appearance, your body language, your emotional state, your visibility, your empathy, and how well you communicate key messages.[3]

While you can't avoid making an impression, you can control the kind of impression you make.[4] As one executive put it: "You need to show up each day the way you want to be perceived—which is simple to say, but difficult to accomplish unless you do your homework and really know yourself."[5] This means that the impression you are trying to make also needs to be rooted in authenticity

Let me ask you:

- Do you spell-check a report before turning it in to your boss?

- Do you watch your table manners when dining with an important client?

- Do you "dress for success" when going on a job interview?

It isn't any *less* authentic to be seen at your best than it is to display your worst (or sloppiest) behaviors. The problem arises only if you confuse authenticity with habit. For example, while you may slouch because you have poor posture, that doesn't make slouching authentic; it simply makes it a habit—and, by the way, not a habit that serves you well as a leader.

Leadership presence is aligning other people's perception of you with your best authentic self.

Building Leadership Presence One Tip at a Time

From my years of coaching politicians, executives, and emerging leaders, I've identified the five qualities at the core of leadership presence:

1 **Credibility:** Are you competent and knowledgeable?

2 **Confidence:** Do you believe in yourself?

3 **Composure:** Can you stay calm and controlled under pressure?

4 **Connection:** Do you relate to others empathetically?

5 **Charisma:** Are you aware of your natural charm?

Yet even if you possess these five qualities and answered "yes" to all the questions, you may still lack presence. To stand out as a leader, you must be able to effectively *display* these qualities in combination with each other. That is why leadership presence is a skill to be developed and why the tips in this book can become your key to success.

Figure 1.1   Five Qualities of Leadership Presence

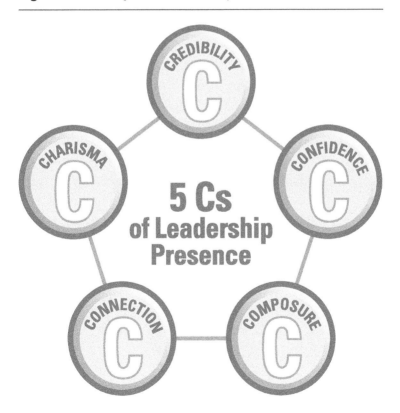

The thought of developing a new skill that incorporates all of these qualities at once may seem overwhelming at first, but the good news is that you can make dramatic improvements to your leadership presence just one simple tip at a time.

Five Simple Tips to Increase Your Ability to Project Credibility, Confidence, Composure, Connection, and Charisma

Credible communicators choose words that have the most impact. The word "because" is one of them. A study at Harvard asked people to break into a line of strangers waiting to make photocopies. When research subjects asked simply if they could use the photocopier ("Excuse me, I have to make five copies, may I use the machine?"), they were successful 60 percent of the time. However, when they added the word *because* to their request ("May I use the photocopier because I have to make five copies?"),[6] they gained instant credibility, and their success jumped to 93 percent.

The next time you make a request, add the word "because" and explain the reason, so that people understand the impact their compliance will have.

Confident leaders send nonverbal signals of power and authority. Tilting your head to one side is a warm signal that you are listening and involved. As such, head tilts can be very empathetic and inclusive. But they are also subconsciously processed as submission signals. (Dogs tilt their heads to expose their necks, as a way to show deference to the dominant animal.[7])

Use head tilts when you want to demonstrate your concern for and interest in members of your team or when you want to encourage people to expand on what they are saying.[8] When you need to project power and confidence—asking for a job promotion or giving a presentation to the executive team—keep your head straight up, in a more neutral and authoritative position.[9]

Sending a nonverbal signal of confidence can be as simple as shifting the tilt of your head.

Composed leaders display poise under pressure. Remaining calm in difficult situations can be difficult, but it is essential to projecting leadership presence. Be careful not to allow a negative expression from the person you're dealing with to trigger unwanted reactions, such as anxiety, self-doubt, and insecurity. When someone frowns or looks disgusted, it's helpful to realize that most of the time, the expression you're seeing reflects more about their state of mind than anything you've done.

To defuse the impact of a less-than-welcoming expression, tell yourself, "It's not about me!"

Leaders who **connect** build strong, trusting business relationships.

When a team member comes to you with a problem, you have an opportunity to make a strong personal connection. One way to do that is with a validating statement.

In doing so, you validate the feelings of your team member without validating the problem—which is, often, all the person needs you to do. Validating statements include:

- "I get it."
- "That makes sense."
- "I can see what a tough spot you're in."
- "I understand why you feel that way."

When a team member comes to you with a problem, connect immediately by making a validating statement.

Charismatic leaders use their unique brand of personal charm to attract others.

Charisma can be described as a magnetic flow of energy—and it often starts with a smile. Humans produce about 50 distinct types of smiles, but there's one distinction that really matters in terms of projecting charisma: Is the smile real or fake? Fake—or "polite"—smiles turn up the corners of the mouth, but genuine enjoyment smiles light up the entire face and create crow's feet at the corner of the eyes.[10]

When you genuinely smile at people, they almost always smile in return.[11] You probably knew that. But did you also know that slow-onset smiles lead to even more positive reactions? So, rather than approaching people with a grin, begin with a slight smile and let it grow organically—until it lights up your entire face and lets your natural charisma shine through.

Facial expressions trigger corresponding feelings. The smile you get back from someone actually changes that person's emotional state in a positive way.[12]

Authentic Leadership Presence Begins with Your Values

To reflect your authentic self, leadership presence needs to be rooted in the values that define you. The "homework" of truly knowing yourself begins with this reflection on your core values and how you express them. See Figure 1.2.

Achieving Your Leadership Presence Goals

Goal setting is the first step of successful goal achievement. Top performers, world-class athletes, and corporate executives all set goals. Goal setting helps you become an active player instead of being a passive observer. When you create a target to aim at, you allow your mind to focus rather than aimlessly wasting mental energy.

1. Write Your Goals as Affirmations

The physical act of writing down goals makes them harder to ignore, and writing them as affirmations turns goals into statements of accomplishment.

Figure 1.2   Reflect on Your Core Values

▶ **List three of your core leadership values.** *Examples: openness, persistence, equality, honesty, compassion, generosity, family-centricity, fun, joy, tenacity, candor, professionalism.*

▶ **Select one at a time and think about why that value is so important.** *Where did you first learn it and in what ways do you currently display it?*

1   Value

Why is it important?

_____

_____

2   Value

Why is it important?

_____

_____

3   Value

Why is it important?

_____

_____

How will developing leadership presence create a truer reflection of your values and character?

_____

_____

> **Action Item**
>
> Don't just write your goals; affirm them. Instead of "I will display more confidence when I speak" try "I speak with increased confidence."

2. Make Your Goals Specific

Identify what you want to accomplish as specifically as you can. Goals that are specific have a greater chance of being accomplished.

> **Action Item**
>
> Instead of writing "I am empathetic," try "I use the skill of empathetic listening to deepen my connection with people on my team."

3. Make Your Goals Motivational

Any goal you set for yourself should be motivating. To make sure of this, write down *why* it's important to you.

> **Action Item**
>
> Ask yourself, "What would I tell other people to convince them this is a worthwhile goal?"

4. Tell the Right Person

In 2009, Ohio State University's Fisher College of Business released a study that found that people are more likely to achieve their goals if they share them with the right person. Researchers saw greater commitment and performance when goals were shared with someone whose opinion was valued or who had higher status—because the goal setters cared about what that higher-status person would think of them.[13] Who exactly is that "right person"? The study, published by the *Journal of Applied Psychology*, says that it has to be someone you see as being "higher in status" than yourself.[14]

Action Item

To utilize positive peer pressure, let someone you respect know what you are striving to achieve.

Written Affirmations	Specific	Motivational	Shared

In addition to writing and sharing goals, here are seven additional tips to achieving your goals using visualization, vision boards, action steps, triggers, rewards, enjoyment, and a growth mindset.

1 **Visualize your goals.** An article in *Psychology Today* looks at how "seasoned athletes use vivid, highly detailed internal images and run-throughs of the entire performance, engaging all their senses in their mental rehearsal. . . . World Champion golfer Jack Nicklaus has said: 'I never hit a shot, not even in practice, without having a very sharp in-focus picture of it in my head.'"[15]

2 **Make a vision board to put your goal in pictures.** Posting and focusing on images that act as visual metaphors for the things you want to manifest help drive your goals deeper in your subconscious.

Start with a big poster board and fill it with images of things that represent your goals: a photo of a leader you admire and would like to emulate, the title of the next job or promotion you are seeking, a sports team that is working together the way you'd like your team to be. Find a symbol for the money you'd like to make, the trips you'd like to take, or the office you'd like to have. Your vision board can be whatever you want it to be, so make sure it represents your highest goals.

3 **Break your goals into action steps.** In a University of California study, researchers had a group of students visualize doing well in an exam, and another group visualizing taking the necessary steps to reach the goal. The results were clear in favor of the group who visualized studying, reading, and gaining required skills and knowledge. They not only did better, but spent longer preparing, focused more attention on the steps needed to reach the goal, and reduced anxiety in the process.[16]

What this means for building your leadership presence is that visualization is even more powerful when you mentally rehearse the actions necessary to reach your goal.

4 **Create a trigger.** A trigger is something that leads you to automatically do something else. To help you create a new habit, attach it to something you already do.

o "As I prepare the agendas for my meetings, I make sure everyone knows why they are invited and how they will be asked to contribute."

o "Whenever I have a one-on-one conversation with team members, I remember to listen with empathy."

5 **Reward small wins.** Early in his career, Jerry Seinfeld decided the way to become a better comedian was to write better jokes. Doing this involved writing a lot of new

jokes. To break that big goal into achievable wins, he hung a calendar on the wall, and for every day he wrote a new joke, he put a red X over that date.

Use a similar method to reach your leadership presence goals. In every meeting you lead or attend, choose one new skill to display throughout the meeting—and find a way of rewarding yourself when you do so. Buy yourself a latte, take a walk outdoors, mentally pat yourself on the back.

Recognizing and rewarding small victories trigger dopamine, "the pleasure hormone," which makes your new habit an increasingly positive experience and builds new androgen receptors in the reward center of the brain, which in turn increases motivation to continue learning and growing

6 **Enjoy the process.** Keep reminding yourself that you already are a credible, confident, inclusive, and high-performing leader. You are in the process of building the skills of leadership presence that help you stand out as the leader you truly are. Treat this process as an adventure. Have fun!

7 **Adopt a growth mindset.** The concept of a growth mindset was developed by psychologist Carol Dweck and popularized in her book, *Mindset: The New Psychology of Success*. A mindset is the point of view you adopt that profoundly impacts how you view yourself. A fixed mindset reflects the belief that your abilities are fixed traits and can't be changed. A growth mindset is based on the belief that your abilities can be developed—and that you are capable of learning whatever skills are required to reach your goal.

When you adopt a growth mindset, you embrace the idea that your best authentic self is always evolving—and just because some attitude or behavior feels more comfortable to you today doesn't necessarily make it a trait you are fated to take into your future.

With a growth mindset, you can minimize whatever development challenges you face by adding the word *yet*:

o "I don't feel comfortable with public speaking . . . yet."

o "I'm not assertive . . . yet."

o "I am not well known in my organization . . . yet."

Visualization	Vision Boards	Action Steps	Triggers	Rewards
	Fun		Growth Mindset	

My Goal for You

You don't have to be born with leadership presence; you can develop it. Throughout my career, I've worked with thousands of wonderful, high-performing professionals and helped them project leadership presence to advance their career. Whether you are an introvert or an extrovert, an emerging or an established leader, you can enhance your communication skills and project your unique style to have a more positive impact.

At its core, leadership presence is a set of skills that you can develop one tip at a time.

Key Takeaways

- Looking like a leader, being perceived as a leader, when you interact with customers, peers, and executives is the essence of leadership presence.

- Leadership presence is aligning other people's perception of you with your best authentic self.

- The next time you make a request, add the word "because" and explain the reason, so that people understand the impact their compliance will have.

- To defuse the impact of a less-than-welcoming expression, tell yourself, "It's not about me!"

- When a team member comes to you with a problem, connect immediately by making a validating statement.

- Facial expressions trigger corresponding feelings. The smile you get back from someone actually changes that person's emotional state in a positive way.

- At its core, leadership presence is a set of skills that you can develop one tip at a time.

2
Credibility

You may be knowledgeable, skilled, and innovative, but that alone doesn't guarantee that others see you as the credible leader you authentically are. Your credibility is evaluated by how well you express your knowledge, expertise, and ideas. In this chapter, I help you sharpen your communication skills so you can more positively influence people's perception of your credibility.

Compelling Communication

One important thing I've learned is that leadership can come from anywhere in the organization, not just the top. Anyone who has a vision of where the company is going and can communicate in a compelling way is a leader.

Compelling communicators are clear, concise, and focused on the results they want to achieve. They tell stories, know when to stop talking, and understand how being vulnerable adds to their credibility.

15 Communication Tips to Project Credibility

1 **Don't just sit there; say something.** At every meeting you attend, make a comment or ask a question early on. This will help you get comfortable talking—and help other participants get used to hearing your voice. Remind yourself that you are at the meeting because you deserve to be and because your perspective is valuable.

 Credibility starts with being present. You won't be seen as credible unless you are engaged and focused.

2 Be concise. Express your point of view in a way that's both compelling and brief. Simplicity isn't just a nice-to-have communication skill; it's a necessity. If you ramble, you lose any hope of holding people's attention. If you can't state your key message in 10 words or less, you're not ready to communicate it to others.

3 Start with the headline. Don't overwhelm your audience with too much detail. Practice structuring your comments as if you were writing a newspaper article. Start with your main point—the headline—and add two or three pieces of supporting information, then stop. For example:

"We need to make sure this kind of problem doesn't happen again. Here are three ways we could do that . . ."

When you need to clarify, use phrases such as:

o "Here's what I mean by that . . ."

o "Here's how we came to that conclusion . . ."

o "Here's another way of looking at the situation . . ."

o "Let me give you an example of what I'm talking about."

4 Add a tag line. After you make your comments, add, "Those are my recommendations. Now let's open the discussion to hear your ideas so we can make a decision on what to do next."

5 **Begin with the goal in mind.** Think through what you want to accomplish and structure your remarks with that goal in mind.

Use the Head, Heart, and Hands Model

- **Head:** What do you want people to *know*? What facts/data/examples do they need to *hear* from you to get your main points across?

- **Heart:** What do you want people to *feel*? What specific emotional *reaction* are you after? Do you want them to feel appreciated/enthused/reassured?

- **Hands:** What do you want people to *do*? What action step do you want them to *take*? Do you want them to buy your product, try the new software, give you suggestions? Whatever you want your audience to do, remember to ask for it in your closing comments.

Figure 2.1 Head, Heart, and Hands Model

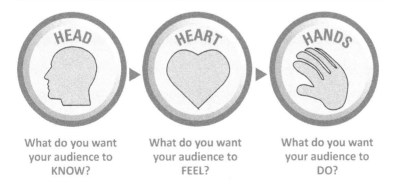

| What do you want your audience to KNOW? | What do you want your audience to FEEL? | What do you want your audience to DO? |

When you use this model, experiment by starting with the HEART or the HANDS first, and see which structure best suits your purpose:

HEAD first: "Here is my idea."

HEART first: "We have this problem/opportunity, and the following idea can help us."

HANDS first: "I'd like you to listen closely to this idea."

Using the Head, Heart, and Hands communication framework ensures that you are engaging on three levels: intellect, emotion, and behavior.

6 Highlight the benefits. Explain the facts and features of your proposal in a way that highlights the benefits for your audience. People are more likely to engage with your message if it affects them directly and appeals to their self-interest. Make sure you are highlighting something they care about.

Remember that your audience will be waiting to find out "Why should I care?"

7 Tailor. You can't be at your influential best as a communicator unless you know your audience. What challenges are they facing? What do they want and need to know? What do they already know about your topic? Different audiences have different challenges, needs, emotions, and knowledge, so you need to find ways to be relevant to whomever you are addressing.

There are two key questions to ask yourself in order to tailor your message: Who is my audience? What do they care about most?

As one company president told me, "My greatest leadership skill is an ability to tailor and craft messages that resonate, whether I'm meeting with truck drivers in the backroom or executives in the boardroom."[1]

When you tailor your message, you resonate with the audience on a deeper level.

8 **Drop the jargon.** While it may seem like everyone uses jargon, don't be afraid to stand out by mastering the art of clear and simple communication. Remember that jargon is industry or profession specific. Credible communicators are those who can speak to and be understood by a wide variety of audiences.

It may come as a surprise that using everyday language can make you more credible. After all, long, fancy words are impressive, right? Well, maybe they're not. The best communicators use language that is easy to understand.

Put jargon aside unless you are sure that your audience understands it.

9 **Replace clichés and buzzwords.** As with jargon, using too many buzzwords or clichés can prevent you from being perceived as credible. Nothing makes a listener's eyes glaze over faster than a leader who overuses clichés like "team player" or "outside the box" or "move the needle."

Instead of "bleeding edge," say "technology so new it hasn't been proven yet." Instead of "let's touch base," say "let's discuss this again at the next meeting." Instead of "our bandwidth," talk about your team's capacity to resolve a problem.

Credible communicators use clear, accessible language in order to engage all members of their audience.

10 Tell stories. Every time I give a speech, audience members come up to me to comment on some story I've told or to share one of their own. The thing I find most intriguing about this phenomenon is that in all my years of professional speaking, no one has ever approached me after a program to say they most appreciated my second bullet point or maybe my fifth bullet point. That's because they apparently don't remember them. But they *do* remember, and learn from, the stories I tell.

Good stories are more powerful than facts. Although facts are critical to establishing the credibility of your message, stories give facts meaning. Good stories make us think and make us feel. They stick in our minds and help us to remember ideas in a way that goes beyond the impact of charts and graphs.

Trying to influence people through analytics is a "push" strategy. It requires the speaker to convince the listener through cold, factual evidence. Storytelling, in contrast, is a "pull" strategy, in which the listener is invited to join the experience as a participant and to imagine the story as it unfolds.

Figure 2.2   Stories Give Facts Meaning

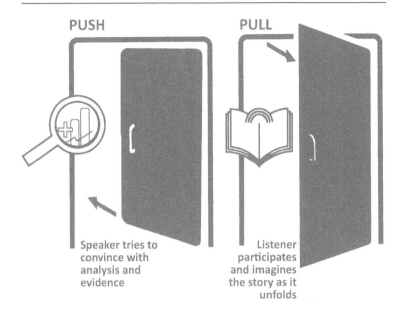

PUSH

PULL

Speaker tries to convince with analysis and evidence

Listener participates and imagines the story as it unfolds

People will remember—and comment on—the stories you tell.

If you already use stories, are you following these guidelines?

o Do you make sure the story is true? (Verify the facts.)

o Do you use the name of the hero/heroine of the story? (People like to hear their names or see them in print.)

o Have you practiced telling the story? (Tell it to your family or friends to get their reactions.)

o Do you use words that help the listener form a mental picture? (Most long-term memory is stored in mental pictures.)

o Do you tell personal stories that reveal your core values? (Few things make you more credible than telling stories that reflect how you acquired your key values and how your leadership style reflects them.)

11 Utilize the power of the pause. Give your audience time to internalize your message by pausing between sentences and before/after making a key point. When you pause before answering a question, it indicates that you are carefully considering your response.

Pauses are effective . . . very effective.

12 Keep people informed. There will be times when you are not at liberty to discuss what you know with your team. Rather than saying "I don't know" when they have reason to suspect that you do, be transparent about the fact that you cannot divulge everything but are sharing what you can. Your candor gives you credibility.

When one vice president I worked with took over a new department, she announced to her staff: "I can keep you informed in either of two ways. I can let you know what is happening as soon as I know anything definite, or I can keep you informed of everything I learn—but you have to remember, some of this information will be sketchy, half formed, and often not totally accurate." Unanimously, her staff chose the second option.

Unlike mushrooms, people do not grow well in the dark. Be sure to keep everyone updated.

13 **Disagree respectfully.** When expressing an opposing viewpoint, avoid taking an all-or-nothing position. Highlight where you agree and be specific about the points with which you disagree. For example, you might say, "While I agree with much of what you said, I do have a different opinion about one of your conclusions."

Respectful disagreement is both empathetic and assertive.

14 **Answer the question.** If you are asked, "Should we post our team's findings now or wait until we have all the results?," your answer should begin with either "We should post now" or "We should wait for results." If you have another opinion, start your answer with: "Neither. We should wait until we've put those results into a formal report."

If someone asks, "Is the project done yet?," answer "Yes" or "No." Then if need be, elaborate on the answer. Don't hedge around because you don't want to answer directly. By saying "The project is virtually done," you're probably not fooling anyone. But if you are, you're also setting yourself up to disappoint them when they realize that you created the wrong impression.

Directly answer the questions you're asked and elaborate only after you provide an answer.

15 **Ask for help.** Organizations exist in a complex and ever-shifting ocean of change. As a result, leaders need to rely more than ever on the intelligence and resourcefulness of their teams. When you acknowledge the expertise of your team members and treat them as true partners, your personal credibility increases.

 Admitting you don't have all the answers and knowing when (and whom) to ask for help adds to your credibility as a leader.

When You Need Backup to Strengthen Your Credibility

Sometimes, when presenting a new idea, you may need to bolster your position by citing an outside source. Being seen as prepared and well informed will build your credibility. You can strengthen your statements by including:

- Examples from other organizations (within or external to your field) that have used a similar idea successfully.

- Business and technical journals that have published articles that support your idea.

- Company publications in which executives who support your position are directly quoted. For increased impact, hand out copies of the quotes.

- Recent organizational data, including charts and graphs, that deal directly with your topic and its value to the organization.

Building Credibility while Leading a Meeting

According to a recent survey, only roughly half of the meetings workers attend are considered productive. Although 35 percent of professionals are in six or more meetings each week, 46 percent of those attendees leave meetings without a clear understanding of the next action item. In addition, missing the information needed to complete projects and prioritizing what to do next were cited as the biggest stressors for workers. And for those who said they are unhappy with their company's management process, the number of people who attend at least six meetings a week jumped to 40 percent (from 35 percent).

These are the findings of the Wrike Work Management Survey of 1,464 professionals throughout the United States and Canada.[2]

When you're leading a meeting, anything you say or do can change the tone, so you need to have a thoughtful, consistent presence. This includes being aware of the impact of your posture and body language as well as the quality of questions you ask and contributions you offer. If you appear skeptical, then a good idea may get shot down. If you appear inappropriately enthusiastic, a bad idea may get implemented.

Love them or loathe them, meetings are a part of corporate life. How you are perceived as the leader of meetings impacts your leadership presence. Here are five tips for enhancing your credibility the next time you lead a meeting.

1 Have a clear objective. Make sure your agenda has these elements:

o A list of topics to be covered (Try structuring the agenda as a list of questions that need to be answered during the meeting.)

o A brief description of what you want the meeting to accomplish

o A list of people attending the meeting (Make sure everyone knows why they are there and who will be addressing each agenda item.)

o The time and location of the meeting (Try starting and ending at odd times: Meeting starts at 9:42 am and ends at 10:27 am.)

o Any background information participants need to know about the subject

A clear objective lets everyone know why your meeting matters.

2 Stand or walk. Your meetings don't always have to be synonymous with sitting. While sitting around a conference table works well for many forms of meetings, an occasional standing meeting can give people a needed energy boost. Walking meetings also have their place. The walking meeting works best when you have a small group; two to three, maybe up to four individuals.

Standing and walking meetings can offer a welcome change of pace.

3 Master your mind maps. Visual aids, in various forms, can be a boost to team creativity. Over the last few years, mind mapping has been used by leaders as an effective communication tool for team meetings. By visualizing concepts and connections in an image, people can follow conversations better and contribute more.

A mind map is basically a diagram that connects information around a central subject. To begin, take a central theme and write or draw it in the center of a whiteboard. From this circle, draw lines like spokes to whatever new ideas are suggested. If one particular idea suggests another association, draw a branch off that idea and write or draw it in.

If you were using mind mapping at your meeting, as people present ideas and concepts, they would simply draw a branch off from the central theme and add that input. You could also draw symbols (like a star) to emphasize important points.

o Write the main idea or central theme in the center box.

o Write each agenda item in the circles linked to the main idea.

o As the meeting progresses, draw lines pointing to subthoughts, ideas, facts, and figures.

o Draw images and interlink items.

Creating a mind map uses associations, connections, and triggers to stimulate further ideas.

Figure 2.3   Master Your Mind Maps

Here is a mind map of this book:

4 Help people contribute. In groups where you've noticed a reluctance to contribute ideas verbally, ask participants to write down their ideas on sticky notes and then display all the notes on a wall or whiteboard. You'll find that introverts respond especially well to this technique.

A critical part of your meeting leader's role is to encourage participation, elicit input, and seek opinions from those who don't readily speak up.

5 Deal creatively with negativity. Leaders gain tremendous credibility when they deal creatively and effectively with team members who continually interrupt or whose negative comments break the positive flow of ideas.

Idea-killing comments include:

o "That's not how we do it here."

o "You may be right, but . . ."

o "I don't think that's important."

o "It's good enough the way it is."

o "That sounds crazy."

o "What a stupid idea. That would never work."

To combat idea-killing comments, leaders use communication guidelines, like the **LCS Technique.** LCS stands for "Likes, Concerns, Suggestions." You can use this tool in almost any meeting, and you will be amazed at how it improves the discussions in the meeting. Here is how it works:

o **Likes.** If you are going to make a comment about something, the first thing you should say about it is what you like. In doing this, you show the person who made the statement and the rest of the people in the room that you understood what was said and that you can identify things you like or agree with.

o **Concerns.** Since no idea or comment is perfect, people often have legitimate concerns about some points in the original statement. Those get stated next, but only if you have suggestions to improve or correct your concerns.

o **Suggestions.** When someone states a concern, he or she must always offer a suggestion to address the concern by adding an idea that makes the original idea better.

Constructive conflict is productive, but negativity is not.

| Clear Objective | Stand or Walk | Mind Map | Write Ideas | Reduce Negativity |

How to Know When You've Lost Their Attention

In business communication, *engagement* and *disengagement* are the most important signals to monitor in your audience. Engagement behaviors indicate interest, receptivity, or agreement while disengagement behaviors signal that a person is bored, angry, or defensive.

Five Signs of Disengagement

1 **Wandering eyes.** We make extended eye contact with people who have our attention. We tend to look away from things that distress or don't interest us, so when people are disengaged, their eye contact decreases. A colleague who is bored or restless may avoid eye contact

by gazing past you, defocusing, or glancing around the room.

2   **Squinting.** Eyes signaling disengagement will narrow slightly. If you've ever seen someone read a contract or a proposal, you'll notice that their eyes squint when they see some clause that is troubling or problematic.

3   **Blinking.** People close their eyes to block out information they don't wish to receive. Frequent blinking or blinking that lasts for more than a second or two is a signal of boredom or disinterest.

4   **Turning away.** When people are engaged, their bodies will be turned toward you, with their shoulders and torsos facing you directly. The instant they feel uncomfortable, they will turn away.

5   **Locking ankles.** When people try to control their body language, they focus primarily on facial expressions and hand/arm gestures. To gain insight into what someone is thinking, keep an eye on their feet. Foot movements are unrehearsed and can be very revealing.

o   When you are speaking with someone who seems to be paying attention but whose feet have turned to point toward the door, realize that the conversation is over.

o   When someone is sitting with his or her feet in a tight ankle lock or wrapped around the legs of a chair, it is a signal of withdrawal and disengagement.

Reduced Eye Contact	Squints	Blinks	Turns Away	Foot Signals

How to Respond

You're leading a meeting—or having an important conversation—and it's going well. And then suddenly everything changes. You're not sure why, but you can tell by their signals of disengagement that you've lost their interest. What do you do now?

Four Ways to Respond

1 Check your position. Are you exhibiting any closed or disengaged behaviors that your counterparts may be mimicking or reacting to?

2 Become engaged. Change your body posture into one of increased engagement, and see if they will follow suit. Lean forward slightly, smile, and put your hands on the table, palms up.

3 Change your pitch. Recognize that what you are proposing isn't being well received and now may be the time for Plan B.

4 Call it out. Bring the disengagement behavior to their attention: "It looks as if this may be a bad time for us to talk. Would you prefer to postpone our meeting until tomorrow?"

 If a person's arms and legs are tightly crossed, hand them something—a brochure, a report, or a cup of coffee—so that he or she must uncross in order to accept it.

Virtual Credibility

Technology has completely changed the way we connect with people to conduct business. It has opened global markets, allowed organizations to communicate effectively despite being geographically dispersed, and enabled professionals to work how and where they can be most productive.

Although virtual communication has advantages, it comes with its own challenges. Communication mediums run a spectrum from "lean" to "rich." A lean medium transmits less information than a rich medium. If you are emailing, texting, or typing in a chat window (all lean mediums), there is nothing that gives added clues to the meaning of what you write. That's why a lean medium is a poor conductor of emotion, humor, and nuance.

With all its limitations, email is still the primary form of virtual communication, and every email you send can add to, or detract from, your professional credibility. If your email is scattered, confusing, and filled with mistakes, the recipient will think of you as a scattered, disorganized, and careless businessperson. If your email is clear and concise, you come across as professional and polished.

Nine Ways to Increase Credibility in an Email

1 **Be specific.** Using a generic subject line like: "FYI" or "Checking in" has much less impact than a specific: "Need suggestions for the agenda by end of day."

2 **Stay professional.** Using "Hey" or "Hiya" isn't professional, no matter how well you know the recipient. Use "Hi" or

"Hello" instead. To be more formal, use "Dear (insert name)."

Using texting abbreviations, such as "u" for "you" in business correspondence, will diminish your credibility.

3 **Keep it short.** People are more likely to read short, concise emails than long, rambling ones, so make sure that your emails are as short as possible and add details in bullet points.

4 **Proofread.** Your email messages are as much a part of your professional image as your presentation skills. Don't diminish your leadership presence by sending out an email full of spelling, grammar, or punctuation mistakes.

5 **Don't overuse exclamation points!** Exclamation points and other indications of excitement, such as emoticons and abbreviations like LOL, should be used sparingly, and only when you know the recipient very well.

6 **Wait 24 hours.** It's never a good idea to send an email when you're angry or in the throes of any strong negative emotion. If you compose an email in anger (or frustration or disappointment), wait a day before sending it. Then read it over and see if it's reflective of how you want to be perceived. In almost all cases, you'll either rewrite or delete the original.

7 **Don't "reply all."** Take time to send your messages to the right people. Send or copy others only on a need-to-know basis. Before you click "Reply All" or put names on the CC or BCC lines, ask yourself if all the recipients need the information in your message.

8 Do reply to sender. If your boss sends you a request for an update on your team's progress, let him or her know you've received the request with a reply such as "Got it. I'll send a report tomorrow afternoon." Because email

messages can get overlooked in the mail or lost in the spam filter, it is a sign of courtesy to let the senders know their message has been received.

9 Sign off. Your signature should tell the recipient who you are and how to contact you. Set it up to automatically appear at the end of each email. Your email signature is a great way to let people know more about you, especially when your email address does not include your full name or company.

Credibility on the Phone

Your voice sends subtle but powerful messages about your feelings. Simply changing your tone of voice can indicate sarcasm, concern, or confidence. In the same way, increasing or decreasing the volume of your voice grabs attention because of the emotion it signals.

People search for vocal clues to unearth possible hidden agendas, concealed meanings, disguised emotions, undue stress—anything, in short, that will help them determine if they can rely on what they're being told.

How to Increase Credibility on a Teleconference

1 Focus. When you allow your attention to wander during a teleconference, you signal that you're not really interested in what is being said. Stay present and focused during teleconferences to retain credibility.

2 Sit up. Even when it isn't seen, your body language impacts your leadership presence. Sitting up, squaring your shoulders, and keeping your head straight helps you sound confident.

3 Stand. Stand, if possible, when you want to convey greater certainty. Standing, or even pacing, gives your voice more energy and conviction.

4 Smile. Smiling while you are talking transmits energy and enthusiasm. When your voice sounds inviting, it draws people in.

5 Make a match. The more adept you are at altering your vocal speed, volume, and tone to match that of the group you are addressing, the better they will hear and accept what you have to say.

| Focus | Sit Up | Stand | Smile | Match |

Videoconferences and Credibility

Videoconferencing can be a powerful way to connect with people, but using it well is a skill that needs to be learned. I once watched a chief executive officer give an entire video presentation bent over notes on a table in front of him while his entire organization viewed the top of his head.[3] When he did glance up, his eye movements looked exaggerated because the camera was much too close to him.

Adding voice and image through videoconferencing offers a great opportunity to enhance your credibility, but be sure you can see yourself and adapt your presentation style accordingly.

Seven Reminders for Your Next Videoconference

1 Get framed. Understand how the camera's distance affects the way you look to a viewer. If you position the camera too closely, every expression and gesture will be exaggerated. You'll get the best results when the screen-image frame starts a little above your head and ends around waist level.

2 Watch your gestures. If you use open gestures, you'll be perceived more positively, but gestures so large that your hands go out of view are useless. Although broad gestures are effective in person, it is better to keep your elbows comfortably in line with your shoulders and limit gesturing when you are on camera.

When not using them to gesture, place your hands on the table or desk, 8 to 10 inches in front of your torso, so that people can see them. Keep them relaxed and separated. Don't hang onto the edge of the table, or you will look desperate. Don't play with your pen or shuffle papers. Make sure to keep a preview window open to check how you look to remote viewers.

3 Make eye contact. Eye contact is hugely important in displaying credibility, but unless you are using a system like Cisco's Telepresence (allowing you to maintain actual eye contact with participants), you have to maintain eye contact by looking at the camera when you speak and at the screen when others are speaking. If the camera is above or below the screen, you might have to adjust your monitor height so that the lens hits you at about eye level. If you use notes, attach them at camera-eye level.

4 Warm up. Participants will be influenced by how likable you are, so it's important to stay relaxed and mentally picture the viewer. Doing so will help you naturally express signals of empathy, likability, and warmth.

5 **Don't get overly emotional.** A bit of a smile is welcoming and will be viewed positively. However, the camera has a tendency to exaggerate everything, so if you smile too big or too much, it will look forced and inauthentic.

6 **Dress for video success.** Colors and patterns appear differently on camera. You'll notice that TV news reporters avoid wearing white because it catches too much light and that they almost never wear clothing with a pattern, because it has a tendency to "jump" and "zigzag." Choose solid pastel or bright colors for videoconferencing.

7 **Watch your posture.** Sit up straight, put both feet on the floor, and take a deep breath. Exhale through your mouth to relax your neck and throat. The goal is to appear at your credible best.

The biggest challenge of videoconferencing is staying aware that every move you make can be seen.

Face-to-Face Is the Richest Form of Communication

In face-to-face meetings, our brains process the continual cascade of nonverbal cues that we use as the basis for building trust and professional intimacy.[4] Meeting with someone gives you the opportunity to express compassion and to directly gauge how well your ideas are being received. In fact, the more business professionals communicate electronically, the more pressing the need for personal interaction.

Almost every effective leader I've interviewed lives by this communication mantra from Caesars Entertainment: "If it's not that important, send an email. If it's important but not mission critical, pick up the phone. If it's critically important to the success of your project, go see someone in person."

When it comes to projecting credibility, nothing beats the impact you make face-to-face.

Key Takeaways

- Credibility starts with being present. You won't be seen as credible unless you are engaged and focused.
- Using the Head, Heart, and Hands communication framework ensures that you are engaging on three levels: intellect, emotion, and behavior.
- Remember that your audience will be waiting to find out "Why should I care?"
- When you tailor your message, you resonate with the audience on a deeper level.
- Put jargon aside unless you are sure that your audience understands it.
- Credible communicators use clear, accessible language in order to engage all members of their audience.
- People will remember—and comment on—the stories you tell.

- Pauses are effective . . . very effective.
- Unlike mushrooms, people do not grow well in the dark; be sure to keep everyone updated.
- Respectful disagreement is both empathetic and assertive.
- Directly answer the questions you're asked and elaborate only after you provide an answer.
- Admitting you don't have all the answers and knowing when (and whom) to ask for help adds to your credibility as a leader.
- A clear objective lets everyone know why your meeting matters.
- Creating a mind map uses associations, connections, and triggers to stimulate further ideas.
- A critical part of your meeting leader's role is to encourage participation, elicit input, and seek opinions from those who don't readily speak up.
- Constructive conflict is productive, but negativity is not.
- If a person's arms and legs are tightly crossed, hand them something—a brochure, a report, or a cup of coffee—so that he or she must uncross in order to accept it.
- People search for vocal clues to unearth possible hidden agendas, concealed meanings, disguised emotions, undue stress—anything, in short, that will help them determine if they can rely on what they're being told.
- The biggest challenge of videoconferencing is staying aware that every move you make can be seen.
- When it comes to projecting credibility, nothing beats the impact you make face-to-face.

3
Confidence

Confidence is the trait most commonly associated with leadership presence. Confidence impresses people, and we admire leaders who have it, but displaying confidence is also one of the most challenging skills to master. Why?

To project confidence externally, you must overcome the internal obstacles to self-confidence. And self-confidence isn't something that you can easily fake.

Think about a time when you needed to project confidence but felt uncertain or insecure. How did you handle it? Did you try to hide these feelings and just fake it till you made it?

If you did, it probably didn't work.[1]

Whenever you attempt to conceal any strong feeling and fake another, your body almost always "leaks" nonverbal cues that are picked up, consciously or subconsciously, by your audience, making them sense that something is wrong.[2]

This chapter offers coaching tips to help you overcome the barriers to authentic self-confidence, convey your confidence in your actions and word choices, and showcase your confidence in formal presentations.

Rating Your Confidence

Read each statement and give it a score (from 1–10, lowest to highest).

1 I think my boss would rate my confidence level as _____.

2 I think my team would rate my positive attitude as _____.

3 People tell me I look confident when I speak. _____

4 I feel worthy of my professional success. _____

5 I acknowledge and celebrate my achievements. _____

6 I ask for new assignments, raises, and promotions. _____

7 I am seen as a risk taker. _____

8 I compliment myself more than I criticize myself. _____

9 People know that I trust my instincts and intuition. _____

10 I share lessons that I've learned from failure. _____

Based on the scores in each category, where are you the strongest and where would you like to improve?

Building Confidence from the Inside Out

Developing self-confidence is an inside job. In order to successfully project confidence, we need to nurture our self-confidence internally and overcome the mental barriers that hold us back.

The four primary internal obstacles to building self-confidence are the imposter syndrome, your inner critic, a negative attitude, and the fear of failure. Luckily, there are strategies for overcoming each obstacle.

Obstacle 1. The Imposter Syndrome

Common among high-achieving professionals, the imposter syndrome is a fear of being exposed as a fraud in which you feel unworthy of your success and are filled with self-doubt and insecurity. As a result of feeling less confident, you may hesitate to offer opinions or push less often than other more confident counterparts for a raise or a promotion.

Strategy: Record Your Successes

To defeat the imposter syndrome, start keeping a success journal. (It's even more effective if you honor and celebrate those successes right after they occur.) At the end of each day, write down all of the things you are proud of, such as goals you achieved and situations that you handled well.[3] Over time, you'll see how even small victories—a productive conversation with your boss, a positive phone call with a client, a meeting with your team that went exceptionally well—when recorded and reviewed on a regular basis, can have a big impact on your pride, self-esteem, and confidence.

 When you shine a light on the ways you are capable and successful, you prove to yourself that you are not an imposter.

Second, learn how to accept compliments and recognition for your achievements. No one gets to your level without talent and hard work. Even if luck played a role in your career, it was no accident or quirk of fate that prepared you to take advantage of the opportunities presented.[4]

 When someone praises you, don't minimize or dismiss the compliment; say "Thank you, I appreciate that."

Third, stop comparing yourself to others. Regardless of how others appear, they likely have similar self-doubts. Virtually every high-potential, high-performing client I coach experiences the imposter syndrome from time to time.

 Just because you can't see other people's struggles and insecurities doesn't mean they aren't present.

Obstacle 2. Your Inner Critic

Of all the negative feedback you may receive, none is as damaging to your self-confidence as your own self-criticism. As one of my clients admitted, "If I talked to my friends the way I talk to myself, I wouldn't have any friends."

Your inner critic notices the things you do wrong or poorly, takes it to heart, and dwells on any critical comment heard from others. As a result, your weaknesses feel magnified and your strengths are ignored.

Strategy: Turn Your Inner Critic into an Inner Coach

Instead of automatically criticizing yourself when something doesn't go well, channel your inner coach. Although your inner critic might say "You are never going to be a good presenter, you might as well stop trying," your inner coach would tell you: "Every time you speak, you learn something that makes you a better presenter the next time. You can do this!"

Become your own biggest cheerleader.

Obstacle 3. A Negative Attitude

When you spend too much time worrying, complaining, and dwelling on the negative, you waste mental energy, sap your enthusiasm and confidence, and make it more difficult to see potential opportunities.

Strategy: Choose Optimism

You can't control events, but you can control your focus and perspective.

In Chinese, the word for "crisis" combines two characters: One is the symbol for danger, the other for opportunity.

Question: Is the glass half empty or half full?

Answer: It's both. It all depends on where you focus your attention.

A positive outlook has long been acknowledged to be a crucial part of high-level confidence. To train your brain to be more optimistic, practice looking for and writing down the opportunities that are within the challenges you face.

Soon you will find yourself automatically focusing on the upside of all situations.

But it takes more than having a glass half-full attitude to display leadership presence. You need to be willing to put that positive attitude into action. This is where I noticed a big difference between passive and active optimists. Passive optimists wait on the sidelines, hoping for the best, while active optimists get involved, persevere, and make things happen.

> A positive, upbeat, can-do attitude is vital for leadership success.

Obstacle 4. Fear of Failure

It is human nature to feel scared when taking on larger leadership roles and responsibilities. But when fear of failure overwhelms us, we procrastinate, avoid taking risks, and avoid operating outside our comfort zones.

Strategy: Fail Forward

I asked a high-ranking leader how she handled failure and setbacks. She replied, "I don't believe in setbacks. I try to fail quickly, learn from it, shake it off, and move forward."

When you know that your failures can't stop you, your confidence soars as you realize that *nothing* can stop you. That's the magic of learning to fail forward.

The "3 Rs" Technique for Failing Forward:

Review: Acknowledge the situation by examining what happened.

Redo: Think about what you learned from this experience and make a clear mental image of what you would do differently the next time you are in a similar situation.

Release: Let it go. This failure has nothing more of value to offer you so release it and move on.

Figure 3.1 The Three Rs of Failing Forward

 You don't have setbacks if you fail forward.

Strategy: Plan a Worst-Case Scenario

One of my coaching clients was being groomed to take control of her family's business. As she explained to me: "This is such a wonderful opportunity. I have so many ideas about how to improve the business. I only hope that I don't let my father down!"

I asked her what would happen if she tried her best and still failed to meet her father's expectations. How would she respond if he didn't approve of her new ideas?

When she replied, "Why, I'd feel perfectly awful!," I asked what she would do after she felt awful.

My client elaborated by outlining an entire sequence of reactions. She fantasized about leaving the area and changing her name and finally joked about putting herself up for adoption. At last she smiled and said, "I guess I'd find a way to survive."

The reality is, you learn more from taking a risk than from staying safely in your comfort zone. When you take on a challenge, you open yourself to becoming more aware of, and growing into, your true potential. And when you realize you can survive the worst possible outcome, you liberate creative energy.

How about you?

1 What is one risk you are currently considering?

2 Why is it important for you to take this risk?

3 If you took this risk and failed, what would be the worst possible outcome?

4 If this approach failed, what would be your other options?

Planning a worst-case scenario reminds you that you can survive failure.

Obstacle 5. Lack of Faith in Your Business Intuition

Have you ever started a project and known what was going to happen beforehand?

Can you sense a problem before anyone tells you there is one?

Do you have flashes of insight about important projects?

Have you ever dreamed the answer to a problem?

Are there days when you do well because you feel especially lucky?

Are many of your best decisions made by going with your gut?

If you answered yes to at least three of these questions, you are already confident about relying on your business intuition. If you answered yes to only one or two (or none) of the questions, you may be overlooking an underdeveloped leadership talent.

Strategy: Increase Confidence in Your Intuition

If you'd like to develop your intuition, start exercising it.

- **Practice foretelling the future.** When you are heading to a business meeting with people you haven't met, guess how they'll look, what they'll wear, and how they will approach the conversation.

- **Notice the feelings you usually ignore.** By monitoring your internal feelings, you are more likely to catch those sensations that indicate something important has registered unconsciously.

- **Keep an insight diary.** Write down flashes of insight and keep a record of decisions you made on that basis. As you reflect on these later, you'll be able to evaluate your intuitive accuracy.

Honing your business intuition increases your confidence.

As you practice these strategies and develop your inner confidence, you will find yourself feeling more confident and able to convey this inner confidence through your actions and body language. Displaying confidence is crucial to leadership presence because confidence and competence are tightly linked. The more confident you look, the more highly people will evaluate your competence.

Three Ways to Display Genuine Confidence

Confidence is often described as the degree to which you believe you can influence a specific outcome. However, you may not always realize how capable you are. If you don't always feel confident, don't worry. No one feels confident in every situation.

If you can't fake confidence, then how do project it when you initially feel hesitant? The three ways to channel and project a genuine confidence include an actor's technique, expansive body posture, and dressing the part.

1 **Become an actor.** Actors often use a visualization technique in which they reflect on their own experience in order to better relate to the emotions of the character they are portraying. For example, an actress who is preparing for a scene in which she needs to display fear may reflect on a time in her life when she was actually frightened. She'd then bring that memory of fear into her current performance.

You can use a similar technique in order to help you prepare for an important presentation. Start by remembering a time when you felt very sure of yourself. Perhaps it was when you competed well in a sporting event or aced a job interview. It doesn't matter if you draw from your personal or professional life, as long as you can picture that past incident clearly in your mind while recalling that wonderful feeling of mastery and confidence. The more visual and auditory detail you include, the better.

Now that you have that image in your mind, visualize yourself presenting at your upcoming meeting with the same high level of confidence and mastery. Imagine how you'll feel, look, and gesture as you make your presentation and how proud you'll be when finished. Your brain can't distinguish between a real and a vividly imagined event, as the same neural pathways are recruited and the same neurochemicals are secreted. The more you repeat this visualization, the more you are practicing success.[5]

Now find a word that summarizes this feeling: maybe "success" or "confidence" or "ready!" You can use that key word as a positive trigger anytime you need to remind yourself that you have had this feeling before, and you can take it with you now.

Each time you repeat this visualization and mentally repeat your chosen word, you come one step closer to making your mental rehearsal a physical reality.

2 Use your body. You communicate a lot about the way you feel through your body—your facial expressions, your posture, whether you hold your head up high or look down. If you're depressed or discouraged, you're likely to round your shoulders, slump, and look down. When you're upbeat and self-assured, you straighten you posture, pull back your shoulders, and hold you head high.

But did you also know that just by putting your body in a compressed or expansive posture, you can trigger the corresponding emotions?[6]

Posture has a powerful influence on the way that others perceive you. It also influences how you think about yourself.

When you physically expand your body, you not only look more confident, you feel more confident.

3 Dress the part. Clothes may not make the man or woman, but your appearance does affect how others perceive you and how you perceive yourself. This is why you are advised to dress with extra care for an interview and why career coaches advise clients to dress for the job they want, not the job they have.

One experiment showed that high-status clothing influences people to respond to you as a leader. When a poorly dress man (scuffed shoes, soiled and unpressed denim shirt) disobeyed the signal when crossing the street, only 4 percent of other pedestrians followed his lead. But when the man was dressed in high-status clothes (suit, white, shirt, tie, shined shoes), 14 percent followed his lead and disobeyed the signal.[7]

In business dealings, appropriate dress is a way of expressing respect for the situation and your audience. This doesn't mean that you have to always wear a suit, but it does mean that whatever you wear should make you feel good, be in sync with the message you want to communicate, and help make the statement that you are an assured and confident professional.

Learn to genuinely project confidence through tapping authentic emotions, expanding your posture, and dressing the part.

People Evaluate Your Confidence by What You Say

Whether you know it or not, you are auditioning for leadership every time you give a presentation, lead or attend a meeting, or have an important conversation. Words count, and the way you use words has an impact on how competent—and confident—others perceive you to be.

Specific words that can make you seem less confident include qualifiers, fillers, repetitions, minimizers, and tags.

Qualifiers

People will judge you as lacking in conviction if you use devaluing qualifiers, such as "to the best of my knowledge," "I could be wrong," "I'm no expert," "This may be a stupid idea."

Action

Drop the qualifiers and simply say "Here's my idea."

Fillers

Fillers, including "um" and "uh," are another communication habit that can make you seem uncertain, even when that isn't the case.

Action

Eliminate the need for fillers by simply pausing between thoughts.

Repetitions

Any meaningless repetitive word or phrase your use—such as "you know," "okay," "right," "basically," or "actually"—is another verbal habit that detracts from your message and makes you seem less confident.

Action

Do you know what your most overused word is? If not, tape record yourself or ask a friend.

Minimizers

When you want to sound self-assured, minimize your use of minimizers—eliminating words like "maybe," "sort of," "somewhat," "kind of."

I overheard this conversation between a manager and his boss:

> Boss: What are you working on now?
>
> Manager: Oh, I'm just . . .

Action

Never say that you're "just" doing something. It makes whatever follows sound insignificant.

Tags

Tags are words you add on to a request: "I need the report today. *Is that okay?*" Or "Please be at the meeting in 15 minutes. *I hope this isn't inconvenient.*" Those tags make you sound less confident.

Action

You can be polite and gracious, but when you need to project confidence, ask for what you want without adding tag sentences that weaken the request.

Figure 3.2   Words That Make You Seem Less Confident

QUALIFIERS

FILLERS

REPETITIONS

MINIMIZERS

TAGS

How to Project Confidence

People judge your confidence based on how you state your opinions, respond to questions, handle interruptions, position yourself in a meeting room, and display confidence through your body language. Fortunately, that's a set of skills that anyone can acquire.

Eight Tips for Projecting Confidence

1 **Make "I" statements.** Each time you find yourself offering an opinion in the form of a question ("Don't you think it would be a good idea to have our meeting next Tuesday?"), stop and turn it into an "I" statement ("I propose we have our meeting next Tuesday").

2 Answer directly. To avoid sounding wishy washy, answer questions directly. Sometimes a simple and definitive "yes" or "no" is all that's needed.

If you were asked how your team could be more collaborative with other business units, you could start with a short answer that gets right to the point and then fill in the details: "There are two ways we could do that. First, we could invite team leaders from other units to tell us how we could better serve them. Second, we could publish a short report of our successes and lessons learned after each project and share that online for other units to view."

3 Interrupt back. If you allow teammates to constantly interrupt you, you lose the opportunity to be a confident and impactful contributor. To regain your ground when someone interrupts in the middle of making your point, interrupt back. Begin by saying the person's name to get his or her attention, then add, "Hold on, please. I'm not finished," or "I appreciate that insight, but you haven't heard my entire plan yet."

4 Own it. Speaking with conviction requires words that carry a sense of ownership and self-reliance. Say "I won't" rather than "I can't," or "I choose to" rather than "I have to."

5 Start small. Sometimes the smallest word choice can have a big impact. One of my clients, an engineer by training, was being groomed for an executive position. As a result, he had been invited to join the senior leadership team. At one of our coaching sessions, he was rehearsing a presentation for this team. When I asked him how he intended to end his remarks, he replied: "That's my report for your consideration." I told him that the phrase "your consideration" implied that he wasn't a member of the team and encouraged him to use "our consideration" instead. My client stared at me and said, "You're right. I'm still talking about myself as someone who serves this team. I need to remember that I'm part of it."

6 **Take a power seat.** Where you sit in a meeting makes a statement about your level of confidence. The power position is at the head of the table, where it's a nonverbal statement that you are the boss. Taking a seat at the opposite end is also powerful.

Another power seat around a board room table is the middle spot on the long side facing the door. This gives you a center position with good visual access to the rest of the attendees.

7 **Let your body speak for itself.** Power and authority are displayed through the use of height and space. If you stand, you will look more powerful to those who are seated. If you move around, the additional space you take up adds to that impression.[8] If you are seated, you can still project confidence by sitting up straight, expanding your arm position (placing them on the arms of your chair or on the table), and spreading out your belongings to claim more territory.

Showing your torso is another way of demonstrating a high level of confidence and security. The more you cover your torso, by folding your arms or hiding behind your laptop, the more it appears that you need to protect or defend yourself.[9] To send confidence signals, open your arms and let your gestures move away from your body.

Feet also send messages about your self-confidence. When you stand with your feet close together, you look timid or hesitant. But when you widen your stance, relax your knees, and center your weight in your lower body, you look more "solid" and sure of yourself.[10]

8 **Assert yourself.** At its core, assertive communication is speaking from an uncompromising commitment to your core values, a sense of purpose, and deep self-respect. It's being able to stand your ground when challenged and to present coherent arguments for why you see things as you do. It's not aggressive; it is clear and straightforward communication that is balanced with an empathetic openness that engages other participants in the conversation.

"I" Statements	Direct Answers	Handling Interruptions	Word Choice	Power Seating
	Confident Body Language		Assertive Communication	

Displaying Confidence in a Presentation

Although public speaking may push you out of your comfort zone, you will rarely have a better opportunity to impress people with your leadership presence. Here's how to showcase your confidence when making a formal presentation.

Tips for Projecting Confidence Onstage

1 **Remain calm.** Do you get nervous before you need to speak in front of an audience? While you want to present with some energy and excitement, you don't want to be so stressed that you come across as nervous or tense.

Before you go onstage, stand with your weight evenly distributed on both feet. Holding your head parallel to the floor, inhale deeply from your diaphragm for six counts. Exhale through your mouth for six counts, being sure to relax your throat.

2 **Show excitement.** Enthusiasm is contagious. If you are excited about what you have to say, your audience will feel it and want to engage with your message. Before you step onstage, remind yourself of how you emotionally connect with what you are about to say.

When you are emotionally connected to your message, it is revealed through your body language.

3 **Present your best self.** Everyone has bad experiences or bad days at work, but it's important to be able to separate what happened in the past from what you're doing now. Before you walk onstage to deliver your presentation, make sure you are clearheaded and present. With your head held high, smile and project the ease and confidence that is part of your best self.

A relaxed, open face and body tell your audience that you're confident and comfortable with the information you're delivering. Reassure your audience with your presence. When you are calm, cool, and collected, your audience will respond in kind.

4 **Grab attention from the start.** As a professional speaker, I know the importance of beginning with something that immediately draws in the audience. You might start with a question, the results of a customer poll, or quote a startling statistic. For a speech on building trust, you

might quote a survey that found 58 percent of people trust strangers more than their own boss.

One of the most powerful ways to begin a presentation is by telling a personal story. Speaking on the need for increased organizational diversity and inclusion, one executive began by describing a work experience in which he was treated as if he were less capable and worthy than his coworkers. He went on to describe how isolated and devalued he had felt and what a devasting effect this had on his personal well-being and productivity.

5 **Maintain eye contact.** Keep your eyes on the audience in order to engage them while you are speaking. Without eye contact, your audience may feel disconnected and distrusting of you and your message.

While you want every audience member to be engaged with your message, it is impossible to look at every audience member at the same time. Instead, focus your attention on specific individuals or small groups briefly, being sure to connect with individuals and groups in all parts of the room throughout your talk.

6 **Ditch the lectern.** Get out from behind the lectern. A lectern not only covers up the majority of your body, it also acts as a barrier between you and the audience. Practice the presentation so that you don't need to read from a script. If you use notes, request a video prompter at the foot of the stage.

7 **Find a metaphor.** Metaphors are figures of speech, a kind of shorthand that makes a statement more memorable by linking it to a familiar visual object or experience.

One of the best uses of metaphor comes from a friend of mine who works as a geophysicist for an oil company and whose job involves interpreting the ocean floor. His job is very complex and difficult to explain, but if you asked Phil what he does, he'd reply, "I draw treasure maps."

8 Use your hands. Your physical gestures can either reinforce or distract from your message. When you are speaking, make sure that your hand gestures underscore the emotion and meaning behind your words.

That's why using a variety of natural gestures connects so powerfully with an audience. When your gestures move out from your body (rather than keeping them tightly in front of your body), you look more confident and engaging.

9 Move, then stop. When you move as you speak, you capture and guide the audience's attention. In addition to hand gestures, moving around helps project energy and excitement and keeps your audience engaged. Underscore the importance of a point by moving closer to the audience as you speak. Indicate a change in subject by turning around or moving away. You can even combine a pause with a purposeful movement to create real impact. Stand absolutely still to highlight your key messages.

10 Use the magic of three. Our brains are wired to recognize patterns, and three is the smallest number needed to make a pattern. The magic of three is a communication technique used by speakers to give their presentation more rhythm and power. Putting your content in triads (as Julius Caesar did with "I came, I saw, I conquered") helps the audience process and retain information more easily.

11 Make it memorable. To help your audience remember your key messages, keep them short. Wordy statements cause listeners to get lost in the words instead of focusing on the meaning. To increase retention, you could also use alliteration, where key words or phrases start with the same letter: "Think about how you can support the company's initiative to *R*educe, *R*euse, and *R*ecycle."

12 **Clarify your main message.** When giving a formal presentation, your job is to make yourself understood. Never take it for granted that everyone in the audience knows what you are trying to communicate. A top-notch communicator follows up important statements with clarifying phrases such as:

o "Here's what I mean by that . . ."

o "Here's how I came to this conclusion . . ."

o "Let me give you an example . . ."

13 **Finish strong.** Make your presentation resonate by finishing with a quote, story, or summary that will easily stick in the minds of your audience. Use this opportunity to remind people why it's important for them to understand or act on this information.

You can also refer back to your opening story. The diversity speaker I mentioned earlier might end his talk by saying "I've highlighted the reasons why diversity makes great business sense: It brings a competitive advantage, higher innovation, and increased profitability. But I value diversity and inclusion for a more personal reason: I never want anyone else to be treated the way I was—or made to feel the way I did."

Manage Stress	Get Emotional	Positive Entrance	Dynamic Opening	Eye Contact
No Lectern	Metaphor	Hand Gestures	Move-Stop	Three Points
	Alliteration	Clarify	Strong Finish	

Building confidence starts by developing a strong sense of inner assuredness—believing in yourself despite occasionally being overlooked or underestimated by others. It is nurtured by positive self-talk, accessing genuine emotions, and increasing awareness of your unique value. Confidence is expressed outwardly and evaluated by how you express yourself verbally and nonverbally in informal conversations, when chairing meetings, and when giving formal presentations. As you practice and incorporate the tips in this chapter, you'll increase your ability to present yourself at your confident best.

Key Takeaways

- When you shine a light on the ways you are capable and successful, you prove to yourself that you are not an imposter.

- When someone praises you, don't minimize or dismiss the compliment; say "Thank you, I appreciate that."

- Just because you can't see other people's struggles and insecurities doesn't mean they aren't present.

- Become your own biggest cheerleader.

- A positive, upbeat, can-do attitude is vital for leadership success.

- You don't have setbacks if you fail forward.

- Planning a worst-case scenario reminds you that you can survive failure.

- When you physically expand your body, you not only look more confident, you feel more confident.

- Learn to genuinely project confidence through tapping authentic emotions, expanding your posture, and dressing the part.

- When you are emotionally connected to your message, it is revealed through your body language.

4
Composure

Have you ever wondered how professional comedians can respond so spontaneously and effectively to heckling or tough questions from the audience?

The truth is that they're generally *not* spontaneous, just well prepared. Anticipating the kind of comments they might have to deal with, comedians rehearse their responses in advance.

Your workplace may not be a theater stage, but staying poised under pressure is a skill worth developing. Instead of heckling, your workplace may present you with unwanted interruptions, tough questions, and personal challenges. These can be difficult situations for even the most experienced leaders. Those who retain their composure and leadership presence anticipate that these stressful events are likely to occur and prepare themselves to respond appropriately.

In order to prepare, it's helpful to understand what is happening in your body when it is under stress—what is commonly referred to as the fight or flight response. Your body responds to stress in myriad ways. Your body releases the stress hormone cortisol. Your muscles contract and you feel tense. You may find yourself short of breath. You may feel your heart beating more rapidly. You may even find it hard to think straight. You are experiencing what is commonly referred to as amygdala hijack. This occurs when the amygdala, which is the emotional region of your limbic brain, overrides the prefrontal cortex, which is the rational part of your brain. Rest assured, these are normal responses to a stressful stimulus.

You can break this link with these five steps: Stop, breathe, affirm, relabel, respond.

1 **Stop.** When you feel these feelings coming on, it's important not let them overwhelm you. Try to retain control by mentally saying the word "stop" to yourself. Taking action by talking to yourself allows you to take the upper hand.

2 **Breathe.** Slow your breathing. Take a deep belly breath, hold it, and then exhale fully. Belly breathing slows your heart rate and gives you more vocal support so that your voice doesn't shake.

3 **Affirm.** Talk to yourself using positive language. Remind yourself that you can get through this, using phrases such as "I'm OK" or "I can do this."

4 **Relabel** as you affirm. As you give yourself a mental pep talk, try not to use intense words such as "anxious," "frightened," or "overwhelmed" to describe how you feel. Be careful not to judge yourself by using negative labels to describe your feelings to yourself. Your feelings are not good or bad—they just are. Remind yourself that having these feelings is natural and a healthy response.

5 **Respond.** Once you have interrupted the trigger-reaction response, you can think more clearly about how to respond. Begin by asking yourself what outcome you want and then decide what action you could take that would most likely achieve that goal.

When you can keep your composure in difficult situations, you appear more confident, which increases people's perception of your leadership presence.

| Stop | Breathe | Affirm | Relabel | Respond |

Preparing Your Response

Now that you have a strategy for interrupting the trigger response, consider how you might prepare yourself to respond to the three workplace situations we mentioned earlier: handling interruptions, answering tough questions, and responding to challenges.

Handling Interruptions

One of my clients grew tired of yielding the floor when she was repeatedly interrupted by a male colleague. Instead of keeping quiet while fuming inside, she decided to prepare a different response. She told me, "I'm going to lean forward, put my hands flat on the table, look at the person directly, and calmly say, 'Tom, hold that thought until I finish what I'm saying.'"

However you choose to respond, preparing and practicing in advance gives you added confidence to speak up when you're in the actual situation.

Answering Tough Questions

When someone asks you a tough question, don't rush to respond right away. Pause briefly to collect your thoughts. A moment of silence sends the message that you are giving the question careful consideration. You can also ask the other person to repeat the question before answering or repeat it yourself. This gives you the opportunity to catch your breath and to ensure that you understood the question.

After you've taken your pause, consider using one of these responses:

- If you know the answer, you can take a breath, maintain eye contact, and then reply.

- If the question is vague or you don't understand it, ask a question, such as "I set out three different options. Which one are you concerned about?"

- You can also paraphrase the question and ask, "Is this the question you're asking? I want to make sure I have it right."

- You can try to restate the question in a neutral fashion before responding, such as "What I hear you asking is . . ."

- If you are unsure of the answer, say "I don't know," or "I can't answer your question just now," or "I need more information before I can give you an answer."

 Before answering tough questions, pause to collect your thoughts.

Responding to Challenges

If you find yourself publicly confronted or challenged, don't rush to respond right away. Again, take a breath and decide how you wish to respond. You can . . .

- **Ignore it.** Simply change the subject.

- **Dismiss it.** Answer in a short, unemotional statement, and move on.

- **Clarify it.** Push it back on the challenger by saying "Before I answer that, tell me how you are defining *unwarranted spending*."

- **Reject it.** Firmly state, "No, that's not the case."

- **Agree with it.** It can be disarming if you say "Yes, you have a valid point. I'll consider it."

- **Discuss it.** If you think the comment needs attention now, bring it to the attention of the whole team and have an open discussion.

- **Control it.** To take control of a challenging situation, start your reply with these words: "I'm not sure this is the best time or forum for us to discuss this." Or if emotions are running high, you can try to distill the anger by saying "I need you to speak to me calmly," "I need you to stop," or "I need you to discuss this with me after the meeting."

Plan ahead by anticipating the five or six most difficult questions you may face and mentally rehearsing how you'd counter them.

Dealing with a Bully

Brenda was the manager of large department in a Fortune 500 company. She was smart, creative, politically savvy, and totally focused on becoming a senior executive.

And she would have reached that career goal if she hadn't also been a bully.

Brenda was a kiss-up and slap-down kind of leader—positively connecting with her superiors while micromanaging, undermining, and criticizing the efforts of those who reported to her. Like many bullies, Brenda was oblivious to the consequences of her behavior. When I warned her that bullying would eventually be her downfall, Brenda dismissed the idea. It was only after she had been passed over for promotion that she understood how her reputation as a bully had ended her career. Shortly afterward, she took an early retirement.

Of course, it was Brenda's team that suffered the most from her bullying behavior. The individual targets of her harassment were especially demoralized, but even those who only witnessed the verbal assaults began to focus more on protecting themselves than on contributing or collaborating.

According to a 2010 Workplace Bullying Institute Survey, 35 percent of the U.S. workforce (an estimated 53.5 million Americans) report being bullied at work, while an additional 15 percent witnessed it.[1]

Bullies verbally insult, demean, and embarrass. They ridicule your ideas and unfairly confront you. Bullies also use body language to signal dismissal, disinterest, and exclusion. When meeting with you, they might continue to read emails, or shuffle papers, or do other work in order to make you feel diminished or unimportant.

I hope you never have to deal with a bully, but if you do, here are some tips to help you:

- Realize that bullying is not about you; it's about the bully's insecurity and need for control.

- Often the best technique is to be direct and simply tell the person to stop: "You are making me feel very uncomfortable right now, please stop."

- Other times, a challenging question works well: "Why are you yelling?" "Why are you accusing me of something that you know I didn't do?"

- If all else fails, find ways to avoid the bully. For some people, that means changing jobs or companies.

When the bullying is nonverbal and more subtle, here are some of the creative responses I've seen:

- To respond to a bully who refused to make eye contact with her, a female colleague stood up and walked to the front of the room in order to command the bully's attention.

- One assistant who felt bullied by her boss hovering and intruding on her personal space decided to turn her chair around to face him and hand him the document he had been reading over her shoulder.

- One team member put gel in his hair to avoid being patted on the head by a coworker who teased him about being short.

 Don't let a bully destroy your composure or kill your self-confidence.

Anticipating the Unexpected

Try this simple technique to help retain your composure in high-pressure situations.

- Make an "unexpected incident" list.
- Then ask yourself what you would do if:

  o your PowerPoint slides malfunction in the middle of your presentation.

  o the 20-minute time slot you had was suddenly shortened to five minutes.

  o you slipped and fell while you were speaking.

  o you were prepared to address one topic and then were asked to switch topics.

 Anticipating the unexpected gives you a sense of control and helps you to maintain your composure.

Stress Management

Stress is basically a response, a flow of energy if you will. "Eustress" is the term used to describe the positive level of stress that heightens productivity, creativity, and enjoyment of life. "Distress" is when your stress levels rise beyond a healthy level and negative consequences begin to take effect. Ill effects of negative stress include high blood pressure, headaches, chronic muscle tension, and the general weakening of the immune system. When are suffering from negative stress over a period of time, your brain stops functioning well and your judgment is clouded. As a result, chronic stress is linked to short-term memory loss and poor decision making.

Eustress increases concentration and focus, resulting in higher levels of productivity, positive feelings of inspiration, and flow. It is where you experience your highest realized potential. Stress control is not the elimination of stress but rather knowing how to pull back when your optimal level of stress increases to the point where it becomes distress and negative consequences begin to take effect.

Avoid Creating Your Own Stress

Most of us say "yes" to requests and assignments without filtering them according to our priorities. The pressure and stress produced by overcommitment can lead to career burnout. Taking on someone else's projects without enthusiasm or interest leaves you less time and energy to invest in those projects that reflect your values and goals.

Knowing how and when to say "no" can be a major challenge. You may fear that others will be disappointed or disapproving if you don't comply. But if saying "no" creates a small disappointment, it's better than saying "yes" and creating a bigger disappointment when you can't follow through in a meaningful way.

Seven Tips for Saying No

1 **Know what matters.** Any decision about how you spend your time requires knowing your priorities are. Before you respond to a request, ask yourself these three questions:

- "Is this an opportunity or a distraction from what I really want or need to be doing?"

- "If I say yes to this, what will I be saying no to?"

- "Is this the best use of my time or do I have higher priorities?"

  Once you are clear about the trade-off you're making, you can decide if it's worth it.

2 **Consider what you're already working on.** Give yourself time to consider whether taking on a new commitment will impact your existing commitments. You might say, "I need to review my schedule. Please send me all the information and I'll let you know my answer on Monday." You will then have a chance to evaluate your current commitments and explain how any new commitment would impact them.

3 **State an alternative.** When your current schedule is full or you are not willing to fully comply with a request, let people know what you *are* willing to do.

- "I'm not available now, but I'll have some open time next week."

- "I won't send your announcement to my entire email list, but I will promote you on social media."

- "I'm overly committed right now. Contact me again next month."

- "I can't stay late on Friday night, but I can come in for a few hours on Saturday morning."

4 **Offer a referral.** When saying "no" to a request, try to think of someone who is more qualified or more suited

to be of help. "Thanks for thinking of me, but I'm not the right person for the assignment. Have you considered Mark? He's an expert in this area."

5 Be direct. Be diplomatic but firm. Don't weaken or hedge your response. Avoid using phrases like "I don't think I can" or "Probably not." Answer directly and succinctly by saying "I'm sorry, but that's not something I can take on."

You may also choose to provide a simple explanation, such as "No. I have a family obligation that evening." Or you can be candid. "I'm rooting for the success of this project, but I have other assignments that take priority."

6 End with a closing statement. To make sure that you end the conversation in a way that doesn't leave room for further discussion, close by saying "Thank you for understanding."

7 Know who's boss. When you need to decline a request by your boss, come prepared with a factual and work-related response, such as "I am swamped with this list of tasks right now. Which one of these can be delayed if I take on the new assignment?" Remember to be respectful, and remember who is in charge. You might want to end your reply with "I understand that this is ultimately your decision."

Developing the skill of saying "no" is critical to projecting leadership presence and achieving your career goals.

Figure 4.1   Just Say "No"

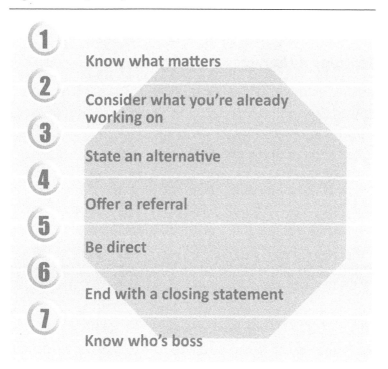

1. Know what matters
2. Consider what you're already working on
3. State an alternative
4. Offer a referral
5. Be direct
6. End with a closing statement
7. Know who's boss

Work/Family/Personal Stress

If you find yourself stressed due to long periods of pressure at work or home, you need to manage your stress levels. Stress control is the manipulation of stress levels; it helps you welcome the amount of eustress that ensures optimal performance and enables you to utilize stress reduction techniques when stress becomes a disadvantage. When practiced regularly, nine stress reduction techniques—reframing, laughter (I replaced humor with this), strategic recovery, counterbalance, healthy habits, flexibility, music, depressurize, and shift focus—can help you combat potential long-term negative effects of stress.

Strategy 1. Reframe the Stressor

How you think or feel or interpret an event can have a powerful impact on your stress levels. If you can change your perception or reframe an event in your mind, it can help protect you from the negative effects of stress.

A study conducted by Harvard and the University of California San Francisco found that people who experienced high stress and who believed that it was harmful for them had a 43 percent increase in the risk of premature death.[2] However, people who were highly stressed but didn't believe that it would harm them had a lower risk of premature death, even lower than people who reported low stress levels. Although further research is needed, the findings from this study indicate that stress may be just as harmful or helpful as you expect it to be.

Strategy 2. Laugh!

The following are a few of the researched benefits of laughter, as reported by the University of Kentucky.[3]

- **Lower blood pressure.** People who laugh heartily, on a regular basis, have a lower standing blood pressure than does the average person. When people have a good laugh, initially the blood pressure increases, but then it decreases to levels below normal.

- **Stress reduction.** Laughter reduces at least four of the neuroendocrine hormones associated with stress: epinephrine, cortisol, dopamine, and growth hormone.

- **Physical relaxation.** Laughter is often referred to as internal jogging in that it has similar benefits. Belly laughs result in muscle relaxation. While you laugh, the muscles that do not participate in the belly laugh relax. When you finish laughing, those muscles involved in the laughter start to relax.

- **Brain function.** Laughter stimulates both sides of the brain to enhance learning. It eases muscle tension and psychological stress, which keeps the brain alert and allows you to retain more information.

Rather than rigidly bracing for all the inevitable pressures that come with your job, remember to bring a sense of humor and spirit of fun to help you roll with the punches. It's worthwhile to download videos of your favorite comedy sketches. You never know when you'll need a good laugh.

Keep your sense of humor and surround yourself with others who laugh, because laughter is contagious.

Strategy 3. Take Time to Recover

When you work out, you break down muscle tissue. When you rest, your muscles recover and build added strength. In order to build mental resilience, you also need short periods of strategic recovery. Set aside time to practice techniques that can help you bounce back in times in times of stress.

Consider incorporating one of these four techniques in your daily or weekly routine.

- **Reflection** allows you to process events so you can learn the lessons that help you improve.

- **Mindfulness** means focusing your awareness on the present moment while calmly acknowledging and accepting your feelings, thoughts, and bodily sensations.[4] A few minutes of mindful awareness in the middle of a hectic day allows you to not be overly influenced by what's going on around you.

- **Visualization** involves closing your eyes and imagining yourself in a beautiful setting that brings you peace or picturing an energizing activity that brings you joy. It is a great way to relax and recharge because the brain doesn't know the difference between an actual experience and a vivid mental image.

- **Gratitude** may be one of the simplest and most effective ways to recharge. Try this exercise for a month and see for yourself the positive effect it will have on your ability to stay centered and calm. See Figure 4.2.

Strategy 4. Find Counterbalance

From art, to music, to sports, to hobbies, to friends and family, you'll deal better with work-related challenges and be more effective on the job when your life includes people and activities that create a personal sense of balance.

A CEO of a cellular telephone company once shared how he achieves counterbalance. "I find counterbalance in my sock drawer. All hell can be breaking loose at work, but when I come home, I open my sock drawer to find everything in color-coded, neat little piles. I don't know why, but it does my heart good." It doesn't matter if the source of counterbalance sounds silly to others as long as it works for you.[5]

Figure 4.2   For What Do You Feel Gratitude?

▶ Each day, find three different ways to fill in the blanks:

| I am GRATEFUL for... | I am HAPPY that... | I am PROUD of... |

M _____ _____ _____

T _____ _____ _____

W _____ _____ _____

T _____ _____ _____

F _____ _____ _____

S _____ _____ _____

S _____ _____ _____

Leaders who strike a balance between the demands of work, home, family, and personal lives are calmer and better able to project leadership presence.

Strategy 5. Create Healthy Habits

The head of Employee Health Services at a Fortune 500 company once shared with me what she believed accounted for the most resilient people in her organization. "The most resilient people in this organization have only one thing in common: They take good care of themselves."

Try incorporating the following health habits into your daily routine.

- **Take a break.** It's been said that sitting is the new smoking when it comes to potentially damaging your health. Those of us who sit in once place for several hours are in the greatest danger.

Make it a habit to get up from the desk for a microbreak once every 90 minutes. Stretch or walk around the office. Even better, take your break outside, as exposure to natural environments is especially beneficial.

- **Follow an exercise routine.** Various studies have shown that exercise influences parts of the brain that regulate stress and anxiety.[6] Regular exercise can increase your energy level and, by increasing the production of endorphins, help produce positive feelings.

Make it a habit to include 150 minutes of moderate aerobic exercise, such as brisk walking, in your weekly schedule. Add resistance exercises for muscle strengthening at least two days a week.

- **Feed your brain.** Your brain requires sufficient nutrients to function well. Limit fast foods, which tend to be high in fat, cholesterol, and sodium.

A protein breakfast with a cup of coffee is a great way to start the day. The caffeine and antioxidants in coffee help your brain by sharpening concentration and may also boost some of the neurotransmitters (such as serotonin) that make you feel good.[7]

Make it a habit to include more "brain food" in your diet, such as fatty fish, blueberries, broccoli, oranges, nuts, dark chocolate, eggs, turmeric, pumpkin seeds, and green tea.

- **Do one thing at a time.** Your brain can only think about one thing at a time. It can switch between tasks quickly (sometimes as fast as 200 milliseconds), but your brain doesn't work nearly as well when you force it to alternate like this. Switching back and forth between tasks may seem productive but, in reality, your performance suffers.

Make it a habit to focus on one project at a time and you'll get into a groove or flow where it becomes easier to maintain or enhance your performance on that task.

- **Get a good night's sleep.** Research shows that anything less than seven-and-a-half hours per night weakens our emotional intelligence and makes us more likely to overreact to stressful situations.[8]

Make it a habit to wind down before going to bed. Turn off electronic devices, take a bath, read books that have nothing to do with work, or think of all the things that bring you relaxation and joy.

Strategy 6. Develop Flexibility

Our organizations today are in a state of perpetual flux, which requires leaders who are flexible, who tolerate ambiguity, who can treat change as an adventure that builds skills and brings forth dormant talents. If you'd like to be more flexible in your approach to leadership, here is a short list of ways to increase flexibility:

- Take an alternate route (or mode of transportation) to work.
- Start a conversation with a stranger.
- Read a book on a topic you've never investigated.
- Learn a foreign language.
- Ask to be cross trained to learn new skills.
- Have lunch with someone in a different department or organization.
- Schedule your day and then purposefully alter the schedule.
- Take an improvisational acting class.
- Engage in an activity that friends say is unlike you.
- Raise children.
- Break a habit and replace it with a new habit.
- Change your mind.

You increase your flexibility every time you try something new.

Strategy 7. Listen to Music

Music can be a natural mood enhancer.

- Give yourself an energy boost by listening to music that has a strong, steady beat.
- Relax by listening to ballads or other soothing music.
- Sing along if doing so makes you feel good.

> Make it a habit to let music help you create whatever mood you choose.

Regardless of how stressful the circumstances, you can control how you manage stress.

Strategy 8. Depressurize the Event

The more importance you put on an event, the more pressure you put on yourself. That's why, if you think of your upcoming presentation as the most crucial event in your career, you're more likely to choke or panic than if you tell yourself that it's just another presentation, similar to others you've given before.

Downplay a situation to minimize the pressure you feel.

Strategy 9. Focus Externally

I am often asked how I handle the pressure of being a professional speaker. One specific question I am repeatedly asked is whether I use a motivational pep talk before going onstage.

Well, I don't have a pep talk, but I do have this mantra: "It's all about them." As I prepare for every presentation, I keep this goal in mind. I find that when I take the focus off myself and place it on the audience, I am more relaxed and less self-conscious.

To reduce the pressure of any performance or important conversation, try shifting your focus from how well you are going over to how well you understand and are serving the needs of your audience.

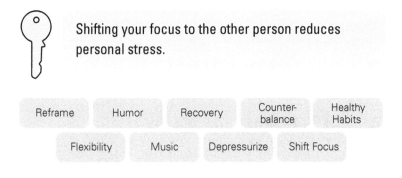

Shifting your focus to the other person reduces personal stress.

Reframe	Humor	Recovery	Counter-balance	Healthy Habits
Flexibility	Music	Depressurize	Shift Focus	

Five-Minute Deep Relaxation Technique to Recharge

Here is a simple technique for getting into a deeply relaxed state of mind:

1 Get comfortable; loosen any tight clothing.

2 Close your eyes and focus on your breathing; make it deep, slow, and rhythmic. With each exhalation, think the word "relax."

3 Become aware of each part of your body, beginning with your face, then neck, shoulders, arms, torso, legs, and feet. Picture your body as a balloon with air slowly escaping until it is depleted and limp.

4 Slowly and silently, count from ten to one and feel yourself relaxing deeper with every descending number.

5 Imagine yourself in a pleasant, tranquil setting—perhaps on a warm sandy beach or in a meadow of flowers—somewhere you feel safe, secure, and totally at ease.

6 Stay in this relaxed state for at least five minutes as you visualize this scene and let your senses explore sights, smells, sounds, and feelings.

7 When you are ready, count from one to ten as you slowly and gently move your fingers and toes, then arms and legs to come out of this relaxed state.

 You can reenergize and recharge in only five minutes.

One of my favorite relatives, Ray, is a firefighter whose profession demands that he keeps a cool head under the most stressful circumstances. What isn't so obvious is the effort and practice it takes to keep that level of control when dealing with what are often life-and-death situations.

The fires you fight at work may be more symbolic than real, but staying poised under pressure is a skill worth developing.

By keeping your composure in difficult situations, you appear more reliable, capable, and sure of yourself—all qualities that increase your leadership presence.

Key Takeaways

- When you can keep your composure in difficult situations, you appear more confident, which increases people's perception of your leadership presence.

- However you choose to respond, preparing and practicing in advance gives you added confidence to speak up when you're in the actual situation.

- Before answering tough questions, pause to collect your thoughts.

- Plan ahead by anticipating the five or six most difficult questions you may face and mentally rehearsing how you'd counter them.

- Anticipating the unexpected gives you a sense of control and helps you to maintain your composure.

- Don't let a bully destroy your composure or kill your self-confidence.

- Developing the skill of saying "no" is critical to projecting leadership presence and achieving your career goals.

- Keep your sense of humor and surround yourself with others who laugh, because laughter is contagious.

- Regardless of how stressful the circumstances, you can control how you manage stress.

- Downplay a situation to minimize the pressure you feel.

- Shifting your focus to the other person reduces personal stress.

- You increase your flexibility every time you try something new.

- You can reenergize and recharge in only five minutes.

5

Connection

We are currently experiencing what is being called a loneliness epidemic, as the last 50 years have seen rates of loneliness double in the United States. In fact, Cigna's recent survey of over 20,000 American adults found that almost half of respondents reported feeling alone, left out, and isolated.[1] From the standpoint of business, loneliness is having a measurable effect on worker productivity and satisfaction. Loneliness is also negatively impacting our health. A recent report posted on the Health Resources & Services Administration website stated that loneliness and social isolation can be as damaging as smoking 15 cigarettes a day.[2]

What does this need for connection have to do with your effectiveness and leadership presence? That's what I'll show you in this chapter.

Here's What Happens When Someone Feels Excluded

Imagine that you are brought into a room to play a computer game. There are three computer screens in the room, yours and two others that show what players in different rooms are doing. All screens have avatars to represent the players in this virtual environment. The game is easy; the three of you toss a ball back and forth. It's also enjoyable, until you notice that the other players are tossing the ball to you less frequently and finally stop including you at all. At this point, you don't know why you aren't part of the game anymore and begin to wonder if it was something you did (or didn't do) that caused the other players to snub you. Later you are told that there were no other players in the game, only a software program that was designed to make you feel excluded. But even when you learn the truth, you are still left with the nagging feeling that this was somehow more personal.

At least that is how you respond if you are typical of the subjects in this experiment by social neuroscientists at the University of California at Los Angeles (UCLA). The research project was designed to make people experience rejection and then to use functional magnetic resonance imaging (fMRI) to find out what goes on in the brain as a result.[3]

The researchers discovered that when someone feels excluded, there is activity in the dorsal portion of the anterior cingulate cortex—the neural region involved in the "suffering" component of pain. So, if you are excluding someone from a key meeting or ignoring their ideas when they speak up, you are causing them real pain.

I've seen firsthand how allowing team members to feel rejected negatively impacts a leader's effectiveness. Those who feel that they are being discounted simply withdraw and stop contributing, and the sense of unease created by that withdrawal then broadcasts itself subliminally to the whole group. And there goes any hope for building the cohesive teamwork that elevates your leadership presence.

In addition, a sense of isolation or feeling of not belonging is among the strongest predictors of turnover. A study analyzing emails showed that new employees who do not switch from "I" to "we" pronouns during the first six months at their jobs are also more likely to leave.[4]

When you let any member feel excluded, it can demoralize an entire team.

The Power of Connections at Work

The goal of leadership is to get others to willingly cooperate and engage rather than following directives simply because you're the boss. As one Silicon Valley CEO told me: "There is absolutely nothing wrong with command and control leadership. It's simply *irrelevant* in the 21st century."[5] That's why your ability as a leader to make genuine connections is so needed and so powerful.

Leadership presence is as much about the emotional reaction you receive from speaking as it is about what you say. That's because emotion gets our attention, and people remember the emotional components of an experience better and longer than any other aspect.

It's important to recognize that all employees bring their emotions to the workplace, and it is those emotions that drive team performance. Leveraging those emotions requires emotionally inspiring leadership.

Here are four simple ways to emotionally inspire your team.

Tip 1. Show You Care

According to recent research by the Center for Creative Leadership, the only statistically significant factor that distinguishes great leaders from mediocre leaders is *caring*.[6] That's why the ability to show that you care is such an important part of leadership presence. Caring leaders make people feel accepted and significant.

 When you show people that you care, you build community and connection.

Tip 2. Share an Inspiring Vision

Sharing a vision is crucial. By "vision," I'm talking about a clearly articulated, emotionally charged, and broad picture of what the organization is trying to achieve and how your team's performance supports those organizational goals.

 A vision gives your team an answer to the question "Why should I care?"

Tip 3. Be a Positive Influence

As a leader, you set the emotional tone for your team or organization. Individuals respond differently to the same statement depending on how it's worded. For example, "We've got a 90 percent chance of success" means the same as "We've got a 10 percent possibility of failing," but people respond better to the positive interpretation. To inspire your team to stay focused, energized, and motivated, choose your words and actions carefully so that you model enthusiasm and optimism.

Be a positive influence by highlighting possibilities instead of problems.

Tip 4. Follow the Platinum Rule

The Golden Rule is "Treat others as you wish to be treated." The Platinum Rule is "Treat others the way they want to be treated." The Platinum Rule requires a deeper connection with and attention to the other person's preferences and emotions. See Figure 5.1.

Follow the Platinum Rule by treating people they way they (not you) want to be treated.

Emotional Intelligence

Emotional intelligence is central to making strong personal connections with your team. How emotionally intelligent are you? Find out by asking yourself the following six questions. If needed, follow the actions steps to improve in each area.

Question 1. Are You a Pygmalion Leader?

In the classic study *Pygmalion in the Classroom*, teachers were given a list of students who had been identified as high achievers and were told to expect remarkable results from them.[7] And, as anticipated, these students performed exceptionally well.

Figure 5.1   Four Ways to Connect Emotionally

It was only after the school year was over that the teachers learned the truth; these children had been selected at random, and not because of any special abilities. Their extraordinary scholastic performance wasn't because they had been identified as high achievers or overtly told they were special but simply because the teachers thought the students were special and, as a result, treated them that way—smiling, nodding, encouraging, approving, and using warm body language as signals of inclusion and acceptance.

As a leader, your expectations of employees/staff/team are a key factor in their performance. If you think people are talented, capable, and special—and if you expect them to succeed—your behavior will display that in how you engage and encourage them. In return, they will most likely rise to your expectations. This effect was described by J. Sterling Livingston in a *Harvard Business Review* article: "The way managers treat their subordinates is subtly influenced by what they expect of them."[8]

After a session in which I discussed this topic with a group, one member shared, "I didn't think much about this topic until I came across a leader who believed that everyone on her team was a rock star. Soon this team that had been struggling to justify their worth to executives began performing extremely well and surpassing expectations. I am still amazed at what this team accomplished because of a leader who believed they were capable."

Action Step

If you are looking to inspire greater performance in your team or organization, you need to provide them with the right motivation. Do you have any processes or rewards in place to acknowledge outstanding work? If not, I'd suggest coming up with a few celebratory ways in which to recognize high performance and then reward your team, even if they are not currently working at the highest level. Feeling appreciated and knowing their hard work will be acknowledged can be the perfect motivation for them to perform at their best consistently.

Question 2. Are You Socially Sensitive?

In researching what makes teams successful, Google's "Project Aristotle" found that their most effective teams exhibited "social sensitivity," meaning that members spoke equally and were able to read emotions based on nonverbal cues. If someone appeared unhappy, others showed concern and support.[9]

Action Step

Pay attention to your team's emotional and physical responses. Watch for changes in facial expressions, eye contact, and postures. When you observe a change, ask a question to see what emotion might be behind it.

"You look uncomfortable. Is there a problem with the proposal?"

"You're smiling. Does that mean you like the proposal?

"I noticed you hesitated. Do you have a concern about the proposal?

"I heard you sigh. Do you have a contrary opinion about the proposal?

"You said you agreed, but your voice sounded strange. Is there some part of the proposal that you don't agree with?"

Question 3. Do You Plan for Difficult Conversations?

Empathetic leaders give lots of positive feedback and make it a habit to "catch people doing things right." However, being emotionally intelligent doesn't mean avoiding conflict or delaying difficult conversations. In fact, conflict avoidance inevitably leads to larger, unnecessary problems and damages people's perception of your leadership presence.

Action Step

Establish guidelines for how team members communicate with each other. Nothing kills a team's creativity and motivation faster than allowing some members to continuously disrupt or derail the meeting. Here's how you might approach a disruptive team member:

- **Start with an encouraging opening statement.** "I am here to (work with you—help you—coach you)."
- **State the specific problem.** "I noticed that in our staff meeting this morning, you interrupted other speakers three times while they were in the middle of offering their opinions."
- **State the impact.** "When you interrupted, the other speakers just shut down, and that killed the creative energy in the room. It was also out of alignment with our team value of making it safe for everyone to speak up."
- **State your objective.** "I wanted to bring this to your attention before this behavior became a habit."
- **State the benefit for them.** "I know you would like to move into a leadership role, and learning how to listen fully before responding is a tactic that will serve you well."
- **State the behavior change.** "In the future I need you to wait until whoever is speaking has finished their thoughts before you comment."
- **Ask for compliance.** "Will you agree to make this change?"

Question 4. Do You Show Appreciation?

Saying "thank you" is a simple but powerful gesture that can lay the foundation for a positive relationship with team members, bosses, and coworkers. Whether it's sending an appreciative email, calling to praise someone, mailing a written note of gratitude, or thanking a person face-to-face, finding ways to point out a person's strength, accomplishments, and support will go a long way toward building connection.

In most cases, regardless of the medium, timing matters: the sooner, the better. Don't wait days or weeks after an event to express your appreciation. Do it right away—and you'll greatly increase the impact of your appreciative comment.

Action Step

Find your own words to express your genuine feelings:

"I appreciate it when you . . ."

"Your advice helped me realize . . ."

"Our conversations mean so much to me because . . ."

"Your contribution to . . . made all the difference."

"You have a unique ability to . . ."

Question 5. Do You Display Vulnerability?

When leaders are perceived as imperfect and vulnerable, team members can identify with those attributes and begin to see the potential for success and leadership in themselves. When you share feelings of vulnerability and when you admit mistakes, people feel safe to also admit errors and ask for help.

Action Step

One of the most powerful ways to display vulnerability is to ask your team for feedback: "What am I doing as a leader that's working well? What would you like me to do differently?"

Question 6. Do You Build Trust?

A client once asked me to evaluate her department and provide feedback on what she perceived as the lack of connection in it. "I think we've lost our foundation," she said. "You know, the foundation for connection—trust."

She was right, of course. Trust is the foundation for real connection, and it's needed on two levels: competence and affect. Competence-based trust happens when you believe that the other person is knowledgeable about a given subject. As a result, you have faith in their opinions and expertise. Affective trust is characterized by feelings of security and faith in the strength of a relationship.

Action Step

Leaders can help build competence-based trust by highlighting the background and expertise of all team members so that everyone sees how each individual's background, networks, and perspective adds value.

Affective trust is built by displays of empathy, concern, and care. It's strengthened by any interaction that deepens personal relationships.

Try this fun and engaging way for team members to learn more about each other. Ask each person to tell two stories. One is a fact about themselves that is unusual or unknown to the group. The other is a lie. The goal for the rest of the team is to decide which is the truth.

Creating Connection in Your Workplace

Ever wonder why when someone near you yawns, you also yawn? Or why you cringe when you see another person getting a vaccination? Turns out, it's your hardwired, natural empathy at work. The moment you see an emotion expressed on someone's face—or read it in her gestures or posture—you subconsciously place yourself in the other person's "mental shoes" and begin to sense that same emotion within yourself.

Empathy helps you understand people's unique needs and judge how to respond appropriately. In addition, it's good for the bottom line. According to Businessolver's 2019 State of Workplace Empathy study, 90 percent of employees say they're more likely to stay with an empathetic employer, and 87 percent of CEOs believe empathy is linked to financial performance. It's no wonder that managers who show more empathy toward direct reports are viewed as better performers by their bosses.[10]

The best way to promote empathy within your team is to model it. Two powerful practices are empathetic listening and psychological safety.

Empathetic Listening

In a research study with over 15,000 leaders across 300 organizations, Development Dimensions International studied the relationship between specific leadership communication skills and overall performance.[11] What the researchers discovered is that empathy—the ability to relate to and understand the feelings of another—is the leadership skill that has the greatest impact on overall performance. What's more, they found that only one in four leaders globally were found to have strong empathy skills. If you already rank high in empathy, you gain a genuine professional advantage. If not, empathetic listening is a skill worth developing further. Here is what's required:

- **Be fully present.** Pay attention. Put away all distractions and focus all your energy on what the other person is saying.

- **Withhold judgment.** Listen with an open mind. Your job is to understand the other person's perspective, not to judge it.

- **Ask questions to clarify.** Asking questions allows you gain greater insight and understanding:

  o "Tell me more about what concerns you about this situation."

  o "What approaches are you trying?"

  o "How do you feel about this opportunity?"

  o "Did I understand you to say (restate what you heard) . . . ?"

- **Ignore the urge to prematurely find a solution.** Not everyone is looking for help. Often people just want a sounding board, someone who will listen while they express their feelings and ideas. So, before you jump in with your advice, make sure they want it. Ask: "What do you need from me? What do you want me to do?" Even if someone wants your guidance, the fact that you have listened empathetically will ensure that you know enough about the issue to be of help.

Psychological Safety

When you make people feel safe and secure, their para-sympathetic nervous systems kick in, giving their immune systems a boost and releasing endorphins that make them feel good. In psychologically safe work environments, team members know that they won't be embarrassed, ridiculed, or punished for speaking up. They feel comfortable speaking up, being themselves, and taking interpersonal risks.

Wondering how to create psychological safety? Here are a few ideas:

- Encourage people to speak freely, and make it clear that there are no stupid ideas or dumb questions.

- Don't shoot the messenger. If you get upset with people for letting you know something is wrong, people will avoid telling you the truth.

- Ask for feedback. When you share an idea or lay out an action plan, ask questions like "What am I missing?" "What am I not thinking of?"

- Don't use candor as an excuse to be mean. Be transparent, open, and direct, but don't be unnecessarily harsh. People like knowing where they stand and what is expected of them, but no one likes being berated or put down.

- Make sure that everyone has the opportunity to voice an opinion and that no one is taking up so much time that others are holding back.

- Thank people for being open and honest.

- Credit the entire team for a successful result.

- When you make an error, own up to it in front of the group and share the lessons you learned.

- Ask more and say less. Instead of speaking first, hold back and ask for other opinions.

- Stay open to what your team has to say about what's working well and what additional resources, information, or support they need to reach their goals.

Empathetic
Listening

Psychological
Safety

Applying the "Yes . . . and" Rule

Connection is built on empathy and inclusion, but sometimes people unwittingly exclude others by rejecting their ideas. Here is where an improvisation technique can help. At the foundation of improv comedy is the "Yes . . . and" rule. Improvisational actors are taught never to contradict their scene partners. Instead, the actor's task is to build on whatever was previously said.

To demonstrate how it feels to have ideas accepted or rejected, I put members of my audience into groups of two (A and B) and ask them to design the next program. They have an unlimited budget, can go anywhere in the world, and include any activities.

In the first round, A offers suggestions. After each one, B replies, "Yes . . . but" and gives one reason why it can't be done. After a couple of minutes, I have them switch roles. This time B offers suggestions and A says, "Yes . . . *and*," then adds one idea that builds on the plan that B is creating.

Leaders gain presence by creating environments where everyone feels they can speak up without fear of rejection or ridicule. This short exercise lets people experience how difficult it is to continue contributing when their ideas are being dismissed . . . and how easily ideas flow when people feel their input is acknowledged and valued. The "yes . . and" rule often becomes the preferred approach to team brainstorming sessions.

 Give the "yes . . . and" technique a try and see how quickly it builds positive connections.

Five Ways to Connect Quickly

With most members of your team, you've had time to create a personal connection. But what about people you're meeting for the first time? Do you have a strategy to connect with them? And can you do so quickly? If not, here are five tips to help you: join their in group, mirror them, pay them a compliment, use their names, and warm up your body language.

1. Find Something in Common

Even relatively small similarities, like rooting for the same sports team or attending the same seminar, can create a bond.

Social psychologists believe that's because people define themselves in terms of social groupings. Any group that people feel part of is an in group and any group that excludes them is an out group. We think differently about members in each group and behave differently toward them. Differences make us a little wary, and similarities make us feel comfortable.

Before getting down to business with someone you've just met, take a few minutes to engage in small talk and look for commonalities that will give you in-group status.

2. Become a Mirror

The most powerful nonverbal sign of connection—and one that you already do subconsciously with people you like, respect, or agree with—is to mirror the other person's body postures, gestures, expressions, and speaking patterns. It's a way of nonverbally signaling that you are connected and engaged.

When using mirroring as a connection strategy, allow two or three seconds to go by before gradually changing your posture or gestures to more accurately reflect that of the other person.

3. Pay a Compliment

If you know in advance that you will be talking with an individual, find out all you can about that person so you can say something complimentary about a recent achievement. Even a superficial compliment will work, such as commenting on an article of clothing. "I like that scarf. It's one of my favorite colors."

The most important guideline here is very simple: When giving a compliment, be sincere.

4. Say Their Name

People love the sound of their name. Calling people by name shows that you care enough about them to invest your time and energy in personalizing your interaction.

When someone is introduced to you, *start using their name right away*, then frequently repeat that name throughout the conversation.

5. Warm Up Your Body Language

Leadership presence is enhanced by projecting authority and confidence, but the "warmer side" of nonverbal communication becomes central to creating positive workforce relationships. Draw people in with warm body language, such as positive eye contact, genuine smiles that create crows' feet at the corners of your eyes, slight forward leans, open palm gestures, and relaxed postures.

Use your head too. If you find yourself in a conversation in which you'd like the other person to speak more, nod your head in clusters of three nods at regular intervals. Research shows that people will talk three to four times more than usual when the listener nods in this manner.[12]

When you warm up your body language, you send nonverbal signals of inclusion and connection.

Figure 5.2   Five Ways to Connect Quickly

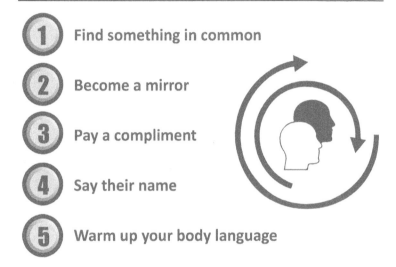

① Find something in common

② Become a mirror

③ Pay a compliment

④ Say their name

⑤ Warm up your body language

As the workplace becomes more automated, the more we want and need personal connections.

Belonging is the brain's key driver, deeply programmed in our tribal nature. Our brains are social, constantly assessing what others may think or feel, how they are responding to us, and whether we can feel safe with them. A sense of belonging is the basis for sharing effort and resources needed to get further faster.

A feeling of connection is at the heart of high-performance teams, manifested in high confidence, security, and trust.

Key Takeaways

- When you let any member feel excluded, it can demoralize an entire team.
- When you show people that you care, you build community and connection.
- A vision gives your team an answer to the question "Why should I care?"
- Be a positive influence by highlighting possibilities instead of problems.
- Follow the Platinum Rule by treating people they way they (not you) want to be treated.
- Give the "yes . . . and" technique a try and see how quickly it builds positive connections.
- Before getting down to business with someone you've just met, take a few minutes to engage in small talk and look for commonalities that will give you in-group status.
- When using mirroring as a connection strategy, allow two or three seconds to go by before gradually changing your posture or gestures to more accurately reflect that of the other person.
- The most important guideline here is very simple: When giving a compliment, be sincere.
- When someone is introduced to you, start using their name right away, then frequently repeat that name throughout the conversation.

- When you warm up your body language, you send nonverbal signals of inclusion and connection.

- A feeling of connection is at the heart of high-performance teams, manifested in high confidence, security, and trust.

6
Charisma

When most people think of charisma, they picture a celebrity making a flamboyant entrance to command the attention of all those present. Although that may be a fitting display of charisma for celebrities, it's not realistic or needed for business leaders. You can exude charisma without being flamboyant, extroverted, or commanding. Max Weber, the father of sociology, first coined the term "charisma" to describe inspirational leaders. Originally from the Greek *kharisma*, meaning "favor" or "divine gift," charisma has also been defined as a compelling attractiveness or charm.[1] I think of charisma as a flow of energy that attracts people to you like a magnet. Charisma is less a quality in itself than a style of leadership presence based on your unique character and talents. The fact is, you already have charismatic qualities that need only to be revealed in order to showcase your unique character and talents.

The Core of Charisma

I once worked with the head of a research department who was preparing for a major business presentation. One on one, this man came across as charming and smart with a great sense of humor.[2] But put him in front of a large audience and he lost all his charm and confidence—in short, he was a disaster.

You may be in a similar situation. When talking with colleagues one on one or leading a team meeting, you may be relaxed and charismatic. However, during important business presentations, you become self-conscious and nervous, and your natural charisma fails to shine through.

What can you do? Rather than trying a new technique, you might be better off simply tapping into your natural strengths, which lie at the core of your charismatic style. Strengthening and showcasing your authentic brand of charisma begins with your answer to this question: How do you best display leadership presence? See Figure 6.1.

Being truly charismatic means being yourself.

Credibility-Based Charisma

If you are a leader with high credibility, your charisma is a reflection of your reputation, experience, and expertise—those qualities that give people faith in the accuracy of what you say. Your charisma is revealed in situations where being knowledgeable and experienced is essential to success, such as strategic planning.

Strategic Planning

Creating a strategic plan requires that you as the leader proactively share your current operating strategy, your knowledge of the business opportunities and risks involved, and any pertinent company successes and failures with your team. Sharing this information requires candor. Rather than

Figure 6.1   Four Styles of Charisma

protecting your team from outside threats, you expose them to your areas of expertise—the complaints and changing needs of customers, the new products of international competitors, and the financial reality of costs and profits. Instead of stifling conflicting opinions, you encourage team members to engage with challenges and problems. You invite your team to join you in a constant questioning of the prevailing business assumptions in order to be ready to support the organization as it acts on new opportunities early in the game to maintain a competitive advantage.

Here are a few questions to get that conversation started:

- What government regulations could change the rules of the industry?
- What new demands/needs could cause our customers to stop buying our product or service?
- What kinds of technological innovation would most drastically affect our product or service?
- What changes (in pricing, services, process, etc.) could the competition introduce that would cause us to rethink the way we do business?
- What companies that aren't our competitors now could become competitors in the future?
- What current competitors could become partners in the future?
- What are the global trends that could most affect our market, both positively and negatively?
- What changes would our team need to make to help the organization take advantage of these possible challenges?

 Credibility-based charisma arises when people have faith in your judgment and guidance.

Confidence-Based Charisma

People are drawn to leaders who display high self-esteem because confidence is both reassuring and contagious.

When you feel confident, you encourage others to embrace risks and take challenges, which elevates their confidence and drives their own and the organization's success.

Risk taking is part of any individual, team, or organizational success. Although inaction might feel safer and more comfortable, failing to take a risk is often the riskiest choice of all. But even the most confident charismatic leaders don't just blindly rush into things and hope for the best. Instead, they are willing to take calculated risks and to encourage others to follow their example.

One of my clients was managing a group of salespeople in her organization who were so afraid of failure that they hesitated to take even well-calculated risks. As a confidence-based leader, she decided to set an example and show them how to take a calculated risk. At the next sales meeting, she put two $100 bills on the table and related her most recent failure along with the lesson she had learned from it. She then challenged anyone else at the meeting to relate a bigger failure and "win" the $200. When no one spoke up, she scooped up the money. She repeated her offer at each monthly sales meeting, and from the second month on, people learned from her example. Her salespeople started to take risks, share their stories at the meetings, and analyze their failures. As a result of this initiative, the sales department grew more successful and quadrupled their earnings in one year.

While it is important to take risks, risk brings the possibility of failure. As a leader, it can be difficult for people to have a genuine discussion about failure that doesn't include blame or rationalization. To facilitate this kind of productive conversation, the United States Army developed after-action reviews. AARs are now used by organizations around the world to provide a safe, structured way to analyze and learn from successes and setbacks.

You lead an AAR process by assembling people who were involved in a planned project or an unscheduled event and ask them four questions:

1 What was expected to happen?

2 What actually occurred?

3 What went well and why?

4 What can be improved and how?

AARs are useful for reflecting on your successful strategies and avoiding future pitfalls. They also send a powerful message that failure isn't a limiting factor if you can learn from it and more confidently move on.

 Confidence-based charisma can inspire others to engage in calculated risk taking, which can drive personal and organizational success.

Composure-Based Charisma

Calm, cool, and collected. If your charisma is based on composure, your ability to stay calm when those around you are losing control attracts others to turn to you in stressful times. Your natural inclination is to take control when circumstances are the most hectic. In a constantly changing environment, where instability must be embraced as positive, people will turn to a composed leader for a sense of stability. That's why a leader's composure is especially needed in times of organizational transformation.

Your charisma shines in business environments that are characterized by volatility, uncertainty, complexity, and ambiguity, or VUCA. Originally used to describe the post–Cold War world, the initialism "VUCA" now is used to describe the current business environment and the leadership required to navigate it successfully. Leaders with composure-based charisma are well suited to guide people through the emotional stages of change: denial, resistance, choice, acceptance, and reengagement.

Denial

Most people and processes are set up for continuity, not chaos. Our brains are wired to defend the status quo, not annihilate it.[3] Not surprisingly, the initial reaction to transformation is usually shock and denial. People in shock are emotionally numb and refuse to believe that the change will take place.

As a leader of the change process, you are faced with the challenge of making sure that your staff understands that the change is important, real, and imminent. It is most important to frankly address the most basic questions:

- What's changing? (And what isn't changing?)
- Why is it changing? (You need to communicate specific information about how the change will positively affect customer satisfaction, market share, quality, or productivity.)
- How can people get involved in designing and implementing the change strategy?
- What new skills will be needed?
- What do people need to do differently?
- What tools/support do they get?

Resistance

Experiencing resistance to change is a result of our neurological makeup. Change jerks us out of our comfort zone by stimulating the prefrontal cortex, an energy-intensive section of the brain responsible for insight and impulse control.[4] But when the prefrontal cortex is overwhelmed with complex and unfamiliar concepts, all of us are then subject to the psychological disorientation and pain that can manifest in anxiety, fear, depression, sadness, fatigue, or anger.[5] When people have moved through the numbness of denial, they usually begin to have very negative feelings.

Resistance is the most difficult emotional component for leaders to deal with, but it's a natural part of the transformation process and must be faced. Leaders need to allow sufficient time for the reality of the proposed transformation to sink in and then create a safe environment for people to express concern and criticism without judgment or fear of the consequences.

Choice

The choice stage is a period of vacillating emotions as people decide whether to support the transformation. I've seen tremendous upheaval in organizations in this stage of transition, as early adapters move into new roles and relationships while other employees stand firm in their opposition.

You help your team choose to accept change by giving them honest information about what they need to do to be successful as the organization changes. It is important to provide examples of other individuals and teams whose behaviors exemplify success under the new model. Sharing real-life examples of success helps make the change real rather than simply theoretical.

Acceptance

Once people have decided to support the change, they are ready for action. The acceptance phase is characterized by abrupt increases of energy and enthusiasm. Informal conversations will begin with: "I've got another idea" and "Where do you suppose this might fit in?" Your main challenge at this point is to focus and channel this energy by restating the overall vision, to give team members access to all information needed to understand the dynamics of the transformation, and to emphasize the need to collaborate with others and experiment with various solutions. It may feel as though you are starting from the beginning of your most basic messages about strategy—and, indeed, in some respects you are. But remember that there is a difference between change and transition. Even though the organization has made the change, your staff members are still emotionally transitioning from their old business environment to their new business environment. The emotional turmoil that the change created means that they probably didn't absorb much until they reached the acceptance phase.

Reengagement

The reengagement phase of the change process is when people emotionally invest themselves in the new structure or organization. This is a time for celebration and rewards, and for finding ways to thank everybody for their contribution.

Above all, reengagement is a time for learning, for helping people realize that transformation is a never-ending process and adaptive behaviors can be learned and incorporated into more effective strategies for the future. The reengagement phase offers a unique opportunity for the entire team to think back through the current transformation to find the strategies, behaviors, and attitudes that were the most effective with this transition to prepare for the next one.

> Composure-based charisma is critical for leaders who are managing in business environments that are volatile, uncertain, complex, and ambiguous

Connection-Based Charisma

The unquestioned authority of leaders in the past has been replaced by the need to enlist all team members as true partners. Your brand of connection-based charisma makes you likable, trusted, and approachable. You know how to talk to other people, how to start a conversation, steer it in the right direction, and make others feel comfortable.[6] Your leadership style is an essential ingredient for success in a collaborative culture.

To further sharpen your natural collaborative leadership skills, here are my A-to-Z tips:

- Show **APPRECIATION** for your team members who collaborate well. Colleagues who help others by teaching and sharing need to have their contributions acknowledged.
- **BODY LANGUAGE** will either support or undercut your verbal messages. Make sure your nonverbal signals support your collaboration goals.
- **COLLABORATE** with your customers. Working with your customers helps to keep your team focused on what is most important—keeping customers happy.

- Celebrate **DIFFERENCES** within your team. Having diverging points of view can help spur new ideas and innovative solutions to problems.

- **EMBRACE** new ideas. Rather than creating barriers to challenging the status quo, encourage creativity by allowing your team to challenge the status quo and offer novel suggestions.

- **FAILURE** needs to be acceptable in order for people to learn. Let the lessons learned from failures and mistakes become the basis for future success.

- **GUIDE** the energies and talents of others while keeping their egos in check. Managing through positive influence and inclusion is much more effective than managing by position.

- **HELP** the flow of ideas by challenging the knowledge-is-power attitude. Knowledge is no longer a commodity like gold, which holds (or increases) its worth over time. It's more like milk—fluid, evolving, and stamped with an expiration date. And, by the way, there is nothing *less* powerful than hanging on to knowledge whose time has expired.[7]

- Embrace new and diverse **IDEAS** and allow them to cross-pollinate to foster creative breakthroughs.

- **JOIN** the celebration. Periodically, take time to celebrate with your team and acknowledge whatever progress has been made to date.

- **KNOW** yourself as a leader. When you are self-aware and know what your strengths and weaknesses are, your natural leadership charisma will shine through.

- **LEVERAGE** the strengths of your entire team rather than simply leaning on one or two high performers. Look across your team to ensure that all members have enough opportunities to grow in their careers.

- **MANAGE** as well as lead. Part of being a good leader is making sure that the business is running efficiently and work is being done—which is a management skill.

- **NETWORK** throughout the organization to enhance collaboration. Encourage your team to build relationships with other functions in the organization. You never know where the next great idea may come from.

- **OPEN** up communication channels. Make sure everyone has access to the information they need or at least know how to get it. You can even create weekly office hours to encourage employees to chat with you directly.

- **PAY ATTENTION** to the details while also remaining focused on the big picture. Collaborative leaders need to be able to switch their focus from macro to micro issues multiple times throughout the day.

- Encourage **QUESTIONS**. Asking questions can help ensure that you are making decisions with all the information you need.

- **RELATIONSHIPS** matter. The success of any team—its creativity, productivity, and effectiveness—hinges on the bonds of its members. Taking time to strengthen personal relationships at the beginning of a project will increase the effectiveness of a team later on.

- **STORIES** remind of us of who we are and what we care about. Collect those motivating and inspiring success and those instructional failure stories in the organization so you can share them.

- **TRUST** is the foundation for collaboration. If you want to create a highly collaborative team, the first and most crucial step is to build trust.

- **UNIFY** your team around its goals. Your team needs to understand the overarching goals of the total organization and the importance of working in concert with other areas to achieve those crucial strategic objectives.[8]

- **VALUE** is created by building collaborative leadership skills. These skills are highly portable, as organizations from high tech to healthcare are shifting to cultures of inclusion and collaboration.

- **WATCH** where people sit. People are naturally reluctant to share information with others when they don't know them personally well enough to evaluate their trustworthiness. If you notice that the same people are taking the same seats at every meeting, rearrange the seating to encourage new relationships to develop.

- **EXAMINE** how people learn. Real learning doesn't take place in the classroom—or in any formal setting. In fact, people have been found to learn more from comparing experiences in the hallways than from reading the company's official manuals or attending training sessions.[9]

- **YOUR** success is dependent on the collaboration of everyone on your team. Everyone contributes to the success of the whole, so make sure everyone on your team understands their contribution. Take the time to remind your team of their accomplishments.

- **ZEST.** Embrace your role as leader with zest and lead your team in learning and developing their collaborative leadership skills.

Charisma based on connection attracts people because you make them feel safe, valued, and supported.

Seven Charismatic Behaviors

Over the years, I've interviews thousands of people about their experiences with charismatic leaders. Regardless of their particular charismatic style, these leaders' positive effect on others can be readily observed and adopted by anyone charged with leading fellow employees at any level of an organization. From those interviews,[10] here is what I have identified as the seven charismatic behaviors of leaders:

1 They encourage you. Charismatic leaders want others to succeed. They possess an almost magical ability to acknowledge achievements and celebrate current victories while continually pushing people to reach even higher and achieve even more.

> Set high expectations and show confidence in other people's ability to get things done.

2 They demonstrate trust. A team's trust in the leader is essential for success. If team members don't trust the team leader, they withdraw and simply stop contributing. But equally essential for success is the leader's ability to demonstrate trust in his or her team. Charismatic leaders take responsibility for choosing the right person for the right assignment, they share information, and, most of all, they openly support, champion, and defend their teams.

> Trust people and let them know you have their backs.

3 **They connect on a personal level.** Most good leaders know which strengths and weaknesses their individual team members bring to the job, but charismatic leaders often know much more: They know what gets someone excited and when things are going well. They know when and why someone may need special attention because of personal struggles. They know which incentives mean the most and whether someone prefers a quiet "thank you" or more public recognition.

Get to know your team members on a personal level and let them bring their whole selves to work.

4 **They include you.** Few people enjoy change when it is forced on them, but most people like change when it's their idea. That why charismatic leaders devote energy and effort (and countless hours) informing, soliciting opinions, and making their team members feel as if they are a crucial part of co-creating something exciting and important.

Include people in designing a strategy and they will embrace it as their own.

5 **They share their values.** The more a leader is willing to be vulnerable, to share his or her values, and to consistently display those values in daily behavior, the more team members can accurately predict how their leader will react under various conditions. Team members also have the opportunity to find alignment between the leader's values and their own.

Share your values so that your team members can align with them.

6 They see themselves as part of the team. The most charismatic leaders don't hold themselves above the job or the project or the exercise or the problem. Instead, they define their role as "a member of the team," and they work collaboratively with other team members to find the best solutions.

Always think of your team as "us" rather than "them."

7 They are highly motivational. Charismatic leaders excite people by a motivating vision of the future based on a solid business case. They understand organizational dynamics and strategy—and they couple that with a deep understanding of human nature based on a high degree of emotional intelligence.

Charismatic leadership is the most motivational when business acumen is combined with people skills.

Figure 6.2   Charismatic Behaviors

Encourage
Trust
Connect
Include
Share Values
Join the Team
Motivate

Key Takeaways

- Being truly charismatic means being yourself.
- Credibility-based charisma arises when people have faith in your judgment and guidance.
- Confidence-based charisma can inspire others to engage in calculated risk taking, which can drive personal and organizational success.
- Composure-based charisma is critical for leaders who are managing in business environments that are volatile, uncertain, complex, and ambiguous.
- Charisma based on connection attracts people because you make them feel safe, valued, and supported.
- Set high expectations and show confidence in other people's ability to get things done.

- Trust people and let them know you have their backs.
- Get to know your team members on a personal level and let them bring their whole selves to work.
- Share your values so that your team members can align with them.
- Always think of your team as "us" rather than "them."
- Charismatic leadership is the most motivational when business acumen is combined with people skills.

7

Body Language for Leadership Presence

Your body language has a tremendous impact on how you are perceived as a leader. When you communicate with others, you can project two sets of cues that impact your leadership presence. The first are empathy cues. People can tell when you are conveying empathy, likability, or warmth through your smile, positive eye contact, open palm gestures, and, most of all, your undivided attention.

Figure 7.1 Empathy and Power Cues

EMPATHY CUES	POWER CUES
Empathy, likability, warmth	*Status, power, authority*
▶ Smiles	▶ Standing or sitting tall
▶ Positive eye contact	▶ Feet hip distance apart
▶ Open palm gestures	▶ Head straight
▶ Undivided attention	▶ Shoulders back
	▶ Expansive gestures

The second set of cues sends signals of status, power, and authority. You display those through your posture—standing or sitting tall with your feet hip distance apart, head straight and shoulders back—and by expansive and emphatic hand gestures, between your waist and your shoulders.[1]

 When you project both empathy and power cues, you are perceived as both caring and confident, which is the dynamic duo of leadership presence.

Conversely, you can diminish your leadership presence by assuming a submissive posture in which your shoulders are rounded, your chest is concave, and your head is tilted down.[2]

 Holding your body in a condensed position not only makes you look vulnerable and powerless; it makes you feel that way too.[3]

Unfortunately, many leaders are nonverbally illiterate. The human brain is hardwired to read and respond to these nonverbal cues, but because some leaders aren't aware of what they are communicating, they are unequipped and unable to use body language to their advantage. Without realizing it, they are sending a multitude of nonverbal signals to clients and colleagues in every business encounter.

But not you! In this chapter, I help you manage your nonverbal communication so you can use body language that highlights your leadership presence.

The Science behind Body Language

Research by the MIT Media Lab shows how subtle non-verbal cues provide powerful signals about what's really going on in a business interaction. These researchers have invented a sociometer, a specially designed digital sensor that's worn like an ID badge. A sociometer doesn't record what's said but rather what *isn't* being said: nonverbal signals and interactions that include tonal variety, vocal nuance, physical activity, energy levels, even the number of smiles and nods exchanged. Based on data from these devices, researchers with no knowledge of a conversation's content can predict the outcome of a negotiation, the presentation of a business plan, or a job interview in two minutes—with over 80 percent accuracy.[4]

But nothing has added more to the scientific validity of the impact of body language than neuroscience and the use of fMRIs. Magnetic resonance imaging (MRI) uses radio waves and a strong magnetic field to take clear and detailed pictures of internal organs and tissues. Functional magnetic resonance imaging (fMRI) applies this technology to identifying regions of the brain where blood vessels are expanding, chemical changes are taking place, or extra oxygen is being delivered. Consider, for example, the research that shows why we like and remember those who smile at us: Using fMRI, researchers found that the orbitofrontal cortices ("reward centers" in the brain) were more active when subjects were learning and recalling the names of smiling individuals.[5]

Good Body Language Goes Bad

Imagine this: You have been standing in a power pose with your feet wide apart and your hands on your hips. As you hold this Superman or Wonder Woman posture, you begin to feel your stress level drop and your self-confidence rise. With these positive feelings and erect posture, you walk briskly into a meeting room where you take your place, standing at the head of the conference table. You speak in a direct and assertive way and make broad, sweeping gestures. You send all the signals of a high-status leader.

The only problem is that the meeting you are going to lead is a collaborative event where you need everyone on your team to contribute, and your authoritative I-have-all-the-answers body language is sending the wrong message.

Now imagine that you are going into another meeting, and this time you remember to display your natural empathy and warmth: You smile, speak softly, nod to encourage others, and tilt your head in the universal listening cue that signals giving someone your ear.

Better, right?

Maybe not, if that second meeting is a strategy session with the executive team, where you hope to be perceived as highly confident.

All body language is "good" when it is appropriate for the situation—and "bad" when it isn't. When it comes to facilitating collaborative meetings, for example, you are more effective when your body language signals are warm and inclusive. So, in the first meeting, smiling, nodding, and head tilts—and even speaking in a softer voice—would have sent positive signals of encouragement and inclusion, as would have sitting instead of standing so everyone would be at an equal height.

But when you wanted to be perceived as assured and confident, a power pose before that meeting could have reminded you to keep your good posture, to speak up early in the conversation with enough volume to be heard clearly, and, when offering suggestions, to keep your head straight (not tilted) in a more symmetrical and authoritative position.

 To make sure that your good body language doesn't go bad, you need to understand what is at stake in any given situation—and adjust accordingly.

How Body Language Is Read

Body language was our earliest form of communication, when the split-second ability to make judgments was often a matter of life or death. Even today, when we have countless means of communication at our fingertips, our body-reading ability is hardwired and based on a primitive reaction that hasn't changed much at all.[6]

There are three constants in how humans read and respond to body language.

1. We Look First for Signs of Danger

Since the human brain is programmed to stay alert for signs of danger, we look for nonverbal warnings that indicate when things are not right. In the workplace, this means that your team members are looking for signs that you are unhappy or displeased. They are trying to figure out how you are feeling by watching your body language.

If you're not aware of your body language, you may be sending signals that are misinterpreted by your colleagues. Your arms may be crossed because you're more comfortable in that position—or you may be cold—but don't be surprised if others judge that closed gesture as a sign of resistance or negativity.

2. We Need Context

Our ability to survive is enabled by our ability to read, learn about, and adapt to our surroundings. In the same way, your employees look for explanations for your body language based on the circumstances in which you work. That's called context—and without it, it's easy to jump to the wrong conclusion. In other words, when the context changes, the same behavior can be interpreted in a very different way. Someone hunched over and hugging herself while sitting outside on a cold day sends a very different message from that same person, in that same position, sitting at her desk: One says "I'm cold!" The other says "I'm in distress."

Sometimes the context isn't so obvious, and your colleagues will need it explained. If you yawn in a staff meeting because you were up early for a business call, let people know why you're tired. Without this context, your team members will assume you're just bored.[7]

3. We Mimic Body Language

Humans learn by imitating behavior. As the leader, any strong emotion you display will cause people around you to automatically mimic your posture and expression. When you're angry or depressed, your negative body language can spread like a virus to the rest of the team, affecting attitudes and lowering energy. Conversely, when your nonverbal signals are filled with warmth and confidence, you help the entire team feel upbeat and energized.[8]

Danger	Context	Mimic

Making a Powerful First Impression

When meeting your new boss, client, or coworker, you have only seven seconds to make a first impression. In that short time, people will decide if you're trustworthy or not, confident or not, credible or not. And they'll have made these judgments based on nothing but your nonverbal cues:

- How you enter the room
- The amount of eye contact you make
- Your gestures
- Your posture
- The sound of your voice
- The expression on your face

Although you can't stop people from making these snap decisions, because the human brain is wired this way, you *can* understand how to make these decisions work in your favor.

Once someone mentally labels you as likable or unlikable, powerful or submissive, trustworthy or devious, everything else you do will be viewed through that filter.

Now that you are aware of how you are nonverbally communicating, you can alter your body language in order to make a positive and powerful first impression. Here are six suggestions.

1 **Adjust your attitude.** People can pick up on your attitude immediately. Before you enter the conference room for a team meeting or enter someone's office for a sales call or job interview, make a conscious choice about the attitude you want to project—and let your body respond.[9]

2 **Check your posture.** Your posture affects how people perceive you. Just as good posture sends nonverbal signals of energy, confidence, and health, poor body posture makes you look as though you are bored, uninterested, or unmotivated. This is probably not the impression you want to project to your boss, customers, and colleagues.

Try rolling your shoulders up and backward while raising your chest. In this position, your head is held higher, which projects confidence and self-assurance.

3 **Smile.** A smile is the most inviting of all facial expressions. It communicates openness and approachability. It says "Welcome, I'm happy to meet you."

4 **Establish eye contact.** Establishing eye contact is a critical component of trust. When you meet someone's eyes with your own, it indicates interest, openness, and engagement. For those who find making eye contact challenging, try to

focus on noting the color of your colleagues' eyes. This will allow you to focus on their eyes a bit longer than usual and helps you to be less self-conscious.

5 **Arch your eyebrows.** When we feel tired, our eyes tend to droop and we look sleepy. If you are feeling tired, revive yourself by opening your eyes wider than normal to simulate an "eyebrow flash." Opening your eyes and arching your eyebrows in this way also communicates interest and acknowledgment.

6 **Lean in.** Your body language communicates interest and engagement. When you are paying close attention to what someone is saying, you tend to lean toward them in order to hear them better. To express interest, it helps to lean forward, but avoid hovering or invading someone's personal space. In western cultures, it is desirable to maintain about two feet of distance between you and the other person in a business setting.

Make a positive impression right away by using nonverbal cues in the first seven seconds of meeting someone.

Attitude	Posture	Smile	Eye Contact
	Eyebrow Flash	Lean In	

Why You Should Talk with Your Hands

The body language question I get asked most often is "What should I do with my hands?" My answer is "Use them."

Neuroscience shows that a region of the brain that is important for speech production is also active when we gesture. Did you ever wonder why you move your hands when you are speaking on the telephone? It is because moving your hands helps you to think and process information more efficiently. When you incorporate gestures into your deliveries, your verbal content improves, your speech is less hesitant, and your use of fillers ("ums" and "uhs") decreases.[10]

Gestures play a key role in how people perceive you. Moving your hands as you speak makes you appear more personable and warm. But if your hands remain still or hang stiffly by your side, you're more likely to be seen as indifferent or cold.[11]

Three categories of hand gestures are used most often.

Emblems

We use emblems in place of words, such as when we use the thumbs-up to indicate "good job" or "everything's fine." Another common emblem is the hand rocking with the palm turned down, which indicates "so-so" or "maybe."

Emblems have an agreed-on meaning, and many are specific to a culture. A specific hand gesture used commonly in the United States to mean "A-OK" actually is offensive in other parts of the world. Be careful of using emblems if you're working in different cultures—you could unintentionally offend your audience.

Illustrators

Unlike emblems, illustrators don't replace words but rather enhance the meaning of what we are saying. We use illustrators when we give directions, as when you point to the right when telling someone to turn in that direction. Another common illustrator is raising your hand or arm to illustrate an upward movement, such as when describing increasing sales.

Regulators

Regulators manage the flow of conversation. When you turn your hand up and curl your fingers toward your palm, it's one way of encouraging someone to speak up. When you gesture toward someone with your palm rotated down, it indicates that you don't want to hear from them right now.

Figure 7.2   Hand Gestures

EMBLEMS	ILLUSTRATORS	REGULATORS
▶ Stand in for words	▶ Clarify your message	▶ Manage flow of conversation

Of course, there are also gestures you should avoid. The most common of these are **pacifiers**. When nervous or tense, you may try to reduce your stress by using pacifying gestures, such as wringing your hands, rubbing your legs, pulling at your collar, or fiddling with your jewelry. In a business setting, pacifiers can make you look tentative or unprepared, so it's wise to eliminate or greatly reduce these gestures.

It is also wise to avoid pointing a finger, as it reminds people of parental scolding and suggests you're losing control of the situation.

And watch out for the "fig leaf." Most of us unconsciously clasp our hands in front of our lower body, creating a protective fig-leaf effect. Whenever you use this gesture, especially during a formal presentation, you seem insecure or uncomfortable. A better choice would be to clasp your hands at waist level.[12]

Gestures are such an important part of your trustworthiness that you should never hide your hands. Instead, keep your hands visible even when seated to show that you have nothing to hide.

 Gesturing helps you appear relatable and can help you connect with your audience.

It's Not Only What You Say, It's How You Say It

Research from Duke University's Fuqua School of Business shows the earning power of a low-pitched voice. The research looked at 792 male chief executive officers (CEOs) and found that those with deeper voices manage larger companies, make more money, and tend to be retained longer. The findings of the Duke study are consistent with recent experimental predictions which suggest that voice pitch plays a role in the selection of political leaders and senior corporate executives.[13] The field of paralinguistics focuses on *how* you say what you say. It includes volume, pitch, inflection, rate of speech, intensity, the use of silence, and clarity.

Paralinguistic cues are crucial to projecting leadership presence.

Five Tips to Sound like a CEO

1 **Breathe.** Tension constricts your breathing and tightens your throat, which makes your voice sound stressed. When you feel tense, try to belly breathe. Look straight ahead with your chin level to the floor and relax your throat. Count slowly to six as you inhale and expand your abdomen, then hold your breath for a count of six, and then exhale for a count of six.

2 **Add intonation.** Intonation is the rise and fall of your voice while speaking. Have you ever heard a leader praise someone in a monotone voice? It's uncomfortable to listen to because it sounds forced and inauthentic. Adding intonation to your speech helps communicate true emotion, whether it is appreciation or disappointment.

3 **Vary volume and rate.** An additional tool is to alter the pitch and volume of your voice throughout your speech. Using vocal variety helps audience members stay attentive and engaged.

  You always want to speak clearly and at a volume in which you can be heard. However, you can use the volume of your voice to give your message added impact. If you are trying to appear more confident, it is helpful to speak a bit louder than normal. And if you are conveying information that is confidential, you may want to speak more softly.

4 **Lower your pitch.** Here's a tip I learned from a speech therapist. Before you enter the meeting room or get on the telephone, let your voice relax into its optimal (and lower) pitch by keeping your lips together and making the sounds "um hum, um hum, um hum."

5 Know when to stop talking. Don't be concerned with filling every moment with words. Instead, try pausing. It's unexpected, it's attention-getting, and it's effective . . . very effective.[14]

| Breath | Emotion | Volume and Rate | Pitch | Pause |

Keeping Your Distance

One of the easiest mistakes to make during a business encounter is to misjudge how much space the other person needs.

I watched a salesman taking a client out to dinner, and by the time they'd finished their drinks at the bar, I knew the deal was lost. Why? The salesman had moved so close to the client as they were drinking that the client began, very slowly, to inch away. Finally the client could stand it no longer, excused himself to make a phone call, canceled dinner, and left the restaurant.

The anthropologist Edward Hall coined the term "proxemics" to describe the five zones in which we feel comfortable dealing with one another.[15] We unconsciously monitor these special zones and automatically adjust as we deal with different people.

How We Use Space

1 Intimate distance, from zero to 18 inches, is reserved for family and very personal relationships.

Figure 7.3   Relationships Inform Appropriate Distance

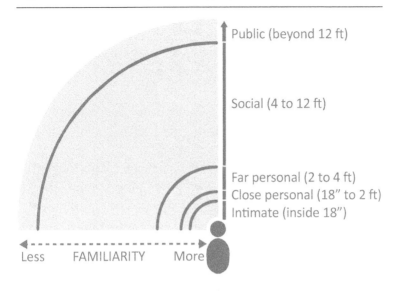

2 **Close personal distance** starts at 18 inches and expands to about two feet. This is the bubble most of us in the United States like to keep around us, even when dealing with friends or trusted colleagues.

3 **Far personal distance,** 18 inches to four feet, is used for informal interactions among friends and business partners.

4 **Social distance** is how we stand at networking events or during coffee breaks at work, when we're less likely to talk about anything personal. It ranges anywhere from four to about 12 feet.

5 **Public distance** is any distance over 12 feet, and it's primarily used when a speaker is addressing large groups.

As relationships develop and trust is formed, both parties almost always move closer to one another. But I've also seen leaders stand uncomfortably close to a team member in order to intimidate or to display authority—which is not a good idea. People's territorial responses are primitive and powerful. When you come too close for comfort, people become stressed and agitated. They'll pull back in an effort to create more space, step behind a barrier like a desk or a chair, cross their arms, look away, or even tuck in their chin as an instinctive move of protection.

It's always best to respect your coworkers' space boundaries by looking for signs of discomfort that tell you you're getting too close too soon. And be equally aware of the positive message you're getting when someone makes that first move to shorten the distance between you.

Mastering the Perfect Business Handshake

In the workplace, we transmit warmth and welcome by shaking hands. Although you may not think twice about it, your handshake may be the greeting that leaves the greatest impression. Why? Because the sense of touch is our most primitive and powerful nonverbal cue.

Your handshake tells others a lot about you. A warm and firm handshake makes you appear confident and friendly, but a weak handshake may mark you as "too timid to be an effective leader." I've also noticed that the "bone crusher"—where a person squeezes too tightly—almost always seems overbearing or insensitive.[16] And when someone offers a straight-arm handshake, creating more distance, they seem distrustful or aloof.

Figure 7.4 How Your Handshake Is Judged

TOO WEAK	TOO STRONG	STRAIGHT ARM
▶ Too timid to be an effective leader	▶ Overbearing or insensitive	▶ Distrustful, distant, or aloof

Ten Keys to a Perfect Business Handshake

1 **Stand.** Always stand when being introduced to someone and when extending your hand.

2 **Free your right hand.** Make sure your right hand is free. Shift your purse, briefcase, beverage, or cell phone to your left hand so you are ready for action.

3 **Make eye contact.** To create a greater feeling of connection, look directly into the other person's eyes as you shake hands.

4 **Smile.** When you add a smile to your handshake, people are more inclined to like and remember you.

5 **Square off.** Keep your body squared off to your counterpart, facing him or her fully.

6 **Extend your hand with your palm facing sideways.** When offering your hand, be sure that your palm is facing sideways rather than up or down. Offering your hand with the palm facing up signals submissiveness while the palm facing down sends the message that you feel superior (because you have quite literally given yourself the "upper hand"). When you offer your hand sideways, you communicate self-assuredness and confidence.

7 **Maximize contact.** Make sure you have palm-to-palm contact—and that the web of your hand (the skin

between your thumb and first finger) touches the web of the other person's hand. Being comfortable making hand-to-hand contact signals trust.

8 **Go for a firm shake.** Shake hands firmly, especially if you're a female. Women with a firm handshake make a more favorable impression and are judged to be confident and assertive.

9 **Talk while shaking hands.** Start talking before you let go of the other person's hand: "It's so nice to meet you." It's even more effective if you say the other person's name: "It's great meeting you, Sarah."

10 **Keep it on the level.** Make sure that when you step back after the handshake, you keep your eyes level. Looking down is a submissive signal. You want your final impression to be positive and self-assured.

The great thing about perfecting your handshake is that you have so many opportunities to practice. Try adding these key elements, one at a time, until you feel comfortable with all of them. Soon it will become second nature, and you will have a perfect business handshake every time.

Reading Body Language for Signs of Deception

As powerful as body language is, using body language to support your verbal messages is only one side of the issue.

The other side—and here is where leaders can really set themselves apart—is the ability to accurately read the nonverbal signals that coworkers, bosses, and clients display in order to respond quickly and accurately to what people are *really* thinking. Peter Drucker, the renowned author, professor, and management consultant, understood this clearly. "The most important thing in communication," he once said, "is hearing what *isn't* said."[17] And nowhere is the skill of reading body language more important than in deception detection.

Your boss seems stilted and awkward as she tells you that "this change is for the best." Is she being honest with you? After a pregnant pause, your colleague happily agrees to help you with your project. Can you trust what he says?

Unfortunately, we don't always read signals and situations accurately. Most workplace lies are uncovered too late and after the damage has been done. But wouldn't it be nice to know when someone was lying to you? Ideally, exposing falsehoods would be as easy as it appears on television shows and in the movies.

Although deception detection remains an inexact science, several nonverbal signals can give you clues into the trustworthiness of the people you deal with.

To sharpen your lie detection ability, follow these four guidelines: Begin with a truth baseline, watch for signs of stress, monitor key body language cues, and look for nonverbal clusters.

Begin with a Truth Baseline

Spotting deception begins with observing a person's baseline behavior under relaxed or generally stress-free conditions so that you can detect meaningful deviations.[18] One strategy employed by police interrogators involves watching the behavior of a suspect while responding to nonthreatening questions. Using this behavior as a benchmark, the interrogators then look for behavioral differences when they ask more difficult questions. If the behavior changes, it may indicate that the suspect is lying.

University at Buffalo computer scientists developed a computer lie detection method that tracks eye movements and blink rates and correctly detects deceit more than 80 percent of the time. Using a statistical technique, they developed a model that reflects how people moved their eyes in two distinct situations: during regular conversation (their baseline) and while fielding a question designed to prompt a lie.[19] It was found that people whose pattern of eye movements changed between the first and second scenario were often lying, while those who maintained consistent eye movement were most likely telling the truth.[20]

In business dealings, the best way to understand other people's baseline behavior is to observe them over an extended period of time, noting their vocal tone, gestures, blinking patterns, and the like. Once you know how coworkers behave normally, you notice when they seem different and their body language changes.

Watch for Signs of Stress

Much of "lie detection" is actually discomfort detection because the mind has to work a lot harder to generate a false response, and that makes most people psychologically uncomfortable. Telling the truth is a more natural response. When you lie, the brain has to overcome its natural urge to tell the truth and then create a lie as well as manage the anxiety and guilt that follows. A heightened stress response is triggered in most people when they lie, which causes an increase in blood pressure as well as an accelerated heart rate and heavier breathing.

To relieve this nervous tension, liars may increase their use of pacifying gestures (rubbing their necks, bouncing their heels, fidgeting with jewelry, etc.). Their feet may rock side to side to self-soothe or even point to the door in a nonverbal signal that they would like to escape. Since our first response to stress is to freeze, you want to pay attention when your usually animated colleague stops gesturing or seems frozen in place.[21] He may be lying.

Additional stress signals include:

- **Under- or overproduction of saliva.** Watch for sudden swallowing in gulps or the increased need to drink water or moisten the lips.

- **Throat clearing.** When lying, the moisture usually present in the throat reroutes to the skin in the form of sweat, leaving the throat dry.

- **Pupil dilation.** Your pupils dilate when you are concentrating or feel tense.

- **Higher blink rate.** When people are apprehensive, they blink more frequently.[22]

Monitor Key Body Language Signals

Subtle nonverbal cues can provide additional support to determine if a person is lying to you, but remember: The best way to read deceitful body language is to compare to a truthful baseline.

- **Backward head tilt.** Liars tend to move their heads slightly backward when they lie. This subtle gesture is an attempt to distance themselves from the source of their anxiety.

- **Moving away.** Another distancing behavior that liars demonstrate is standing farther away from you or leaning back if seated.

- **Narrowing stance.** When being truthful, people tend to take a wider and more deliberate stance. Liars who feel insecure about what they are saying bring their feet closer together.

- **Touching the suprasternal notch.** This is the indentation at the base of the neck, and it's one of the most vulnerable parts of the body. When liars feel threatened, they sometimes cover their suprasternal notch to psychologically protect themselves.

- **Nose touching.** People may unconsciously rub their noses when they are about to lie. (This is most likely because a rush of adrenaline opens the capillaries and makes noses itch.[23])

- **Microexpressions.** Strong emotions can prompt microexpressions, even if a person is trying hard to conceal how they are feeling. Microexpressions are difficult to catch because they happen so quickly, but those instantaneous flashes of anger, dismay, or joy are accurate indicators of someone's genuine emotional state.[24] When in doubt, it's wise to believe what you see, not what you hear.

- **The quick-check glance.** This generally follows a less-than-truthful response: Liars will immediately look down and away, then back at you for a brief glimpse to see if you bought the falsehood.

- **Unusual response times.** Someone who is lying may begin to provide an answer to a question more quickly than someone who is telling the truth. If taken by surprise, however, the liar takes longer to respond, as the process of inhibiting the truth and creating a lie takes extra time.

- **Artificial emotions.** If people's reactions seem a bit over-done, they may be lying. Any facial expression that is held for more than five to ten seconds is almost certainly fake.

Look for Nonverbal Clusters

There is a growing consensus that the idea of a single non-verbal signal of trustworthiness—or deceit—is simplistic. Rather than that one isolated gesture or facial expression, scientists find that deceivers send a cluster of signals that are displayed organically during brief encounters.

That's the idea behind research from psychological scientist David DeSteno of Northeastern University. Working with a large team of collaborators at MIT, Cornell, and his own university, DeSteno ran a two-part experiment aimed to identify the intertwined nonverbal cues that warn of oppor-tunism and untrustworthiness.[25]

In an experiment designed around an economic game, where trustworthiness was a significant factor, four specific non-verbal behaviors tended to predict untrustworthiness. I call them the Telltale Four. They are:

1 Hand touching

2 Face touching

3 Crossing arms

4 Leaning away

Baseline	Stress Signals	Body Language	Clusters

Staying alert for body language cues can help you spot bluffing or deception.

Why Deception Detection Isn't Easy

As I previously stated, the act of lying triggers a heightened and observable stress response in most people. But this is not always the case, which is why deception detection remains difficult.

- Not all people express emotions to the same degree.
- Not all liars (especially if polished or pathological) show any signs of stress or guilt.[26]
- Not all lies trigger a stress reaction. (Social lies—"I'd be happy to attend your meeting," for example—are so much a part of daily life that they hardly ever distress the sender.)
- Not all stress signals indicate a lie.[27] Some people display anxiety not because they are lying but because they are embarrassed about the topic or aren't comfortable speaking in public.

Our own biases may also make it difficult for us to detect when someone is lying. Research shows that our ability to judge whether someone is lying may be affected by factors such as what they wear, what their voices sound like, if they flatter us, or if they are attractive and charming.[28]

When you put your trust in a deceptive coworker or hire someone you haven't properly investigated, it may not be due to their skill as a liar but more about your unconscious biases, vanities, and desires.[29]

The Biggest Body Language Myth

I couldn't close a chapter on body language without mentioning its biggest myth: A classic study by Dr. Albert Mehrabian is often misquoted as saying that the total impact of a message is based on 7 percent words used; 38 percent tone of voice, volume, rate of speech, vocal pitch; and 55 percent facial expressions, hand gestures, postures, and other forms of body language. But Mehrabian's research was focused on the communication of *emotions*—specifically, liking and disliking.[30] Although nonverbal gestures can reveal what you're feeling and thinking, they can't be relied on to communicate the entirety of your message.[31]

People will evaluate the emotional content of your message primarily through your body language and tone of voice.

Body language has played a crucial part in your career—from your first job interview to your current leadership position. You're always communicating both verbally and nonverbally. And when it comes to convincing people of your true intent, your body language sends the stronger message.

The more you know about using body language effectively, the more you will look like the competent and compassionate leader you truly are.

Key Takeaways

- When you project both empathy and power cues, you are perceived as both caring and confident, which is the dynamic duo of leadership presence.

- Holding your body in a condensed position not only makes you look vulnerable and powerless; it makes you feel that way too.

- Once someone mentally labels you as likable or unlikable, powerful or submissive, trustworthy or devious, everything else you do will be viewed through that filter.

- To make sure that your good body language doesn't go bad, you need to understand what is at stake in any given situation—and adjust accordingly.

- Make a positive impression right away by using nonverbal cues in the first seven seconds of meeting someone.

- Gesturing helps you appear relatable and can help you connect with your audience.

- Staying alert for body language cues can help you spot bluffing or deception.

- When you put your trust in a deceptive coworker or hire someone you haven't properly investigated, it may not be due to their skill as a liar but more about your unconscious biases, vanities, and desires.

- People will evaluate the emotional content of your message primarily through your body language and tone of voice.

- The more you know about using body language effectively, the more you will look like the competent and compassionate leader you truly are.

8
Self-Promotion

Hard work and great results are essential, but they won't automatically give you leadership presence. As gifted as you are, your leadership presence can be built only by getting out there and letting others see you in action. Self-promotion is about making sure that others know what you've done and what you are capable of doing next.

How visible are you? Are the senior managers and executives in your company aware of your talents and accomplishments? Or do you believe that working hard, keeping quiet, and waiting for your talents to be discovered is the path to success? If so, take a tip from a savvy leader I interviewed:

> If you want to be evaluated as having leadership presence, then being a legend in your own mind is not enough. Instead, you need to make sure that executives in your company are aware of your work and accomplishments—and you need to do so in a way that is not seen as boasting but as informative and helpful.
> —Dana Simberkoff, Chief Risk, Privacy, and Information Security Officer at AvePoint

This chapter will help you create a plan for self-promotion. You'll learn how volunteering to assist with key projects, offering to lead training, or taking a leadership role in your profession's association can help to elevate your visibility.

You can also look for assistance from your mentors and other sponsors who can help promote you to their peers.

Creating Your Authentic Brand

A company's brand communicates who it is, what it stands for, and the values it embraces. A personal brand serves a similar function for an individual, except that it works to communicate your unique identity, personal values, and greatest strengths.

The basis for creating your authentic brand begins with the answers to these six questions:

1 **What makes you unique?** What is it about what you do, or how you do it, that makes you distinct and special?

2 **What is your purpose?** Why are you here? How does being a leader serve your purpose?

3 **What are your goals?** Where would you like to be and what would you like to be doing in six months? In one year? In five years?

4 **What's your story?** Why do you do what you do? What's the essential story that brought you to this profession, organization, current role?

5 **What are your greatest strengths?** What skills and abilities can people count on you to contribute?

6 **What are you most passionate about?** What activities, interests, situations, and challenges fascinate or excite you?

If you don't create your own brand, other people will do it for you.

Increasing Visibility

In a 2016 study, 240 senior leaders of a Silicon Valley technology company were asked to identify the most critical factors for success at their level. The group agreed on track record and skills-based factors, such as a history of delivering results, technical depth of expertise, and the ability to manage a technical team.

However, when asked them to name the most critical factors for promotion to their level, a new top criterion appeared: visibility. More than technical competence, business results, or team leadership ability, these leaders all agreed that visibility was the most important factor for advancement.[1]

The more someone hears from you or about you, the more they will feel comfortable with you. It's called the mere exposure effect. Simply put, the more visible you are, the more likable and promotable you become.

Ten Tips for Building Your Visibility

1 **Add a photo to your email signature.** This is the simplest way to instantly increase your visibility. One manager who added a photo above his email signature reported that when he walked down the hallway, people he'd never met before greeted him by name.

2 **Speak up.** There's no better way to showcase your expertise and increase your visibility than to literally speak up in meetings and other public forums. Not only is public speaking impactful but sharing what you know serves others.

Offer to summarize your project's progress to the leadership team or submit a proposal to speak at a session or on a panel at an industry conference. Or if you don't wish to present at an industry conference, you can offer to host a brown bag luncheon session where you share what you learned at a seminar or training.

3 **Interact with executives.** Approach executives at office parties and thank them for hosting the event. When an executive holds a meeting, ask questions and email follow-up queries or remarks.

Many of my clients meet executives and other business contacts through sporting events, such as golf. The special appeal of a golf game is that you're with someone for four or five hours, so the conversation goes way beyond a generic "How are things going?"

4 **Work on a cross-functional team.** Working on a cross-functional team gives you exposure to those outside of your own work area and provides an opportunity for them to recognize your talents. Having this exposure and these contacts is valuable when promotions or lateral opportunities arise.

5 **Take advantage of your performance review.** Your performance review is the perfect time to ensure that your manager sees you as the successful and competent professional you really are. Come prepared with a list of accomplishments, projects completed, challenges overcome, and feedback from peers and direct reports.

6 **Know when to brag.** A woman who attended one of my seminars told me about a job interview where she was competing against three men who were well known to the interviewing committee. Since she had recently transferred to the office, a colleague offered her the

following advice: "You are going to see a lot of blank faces because these interviewers don't know you or what to expect if you were given an opportunity. To convince them, you need to brag about everything—the schools you went to, the degrees you earned, the results you achieved in your last position, your qualifications for this job, and anything else you can think of that would help them know how good you are." She followed this advice, and although that particular job went to one of the better-known candidates, the senior team ended up created a brand-new position just for her.

7 **Publicize your successes and those of your team.** Offer to submit a story to your corporate communications department on the successes—or lessons learned from failures—of your team. You may be surprised how much these examples are valued. If the stories are compelling enough, they can be picked up and retold by executives at internal and external events.

8 **Position yourself as an expert.** You'll find that as you develop expertise in an area or for a particular product, service, or process, people will come to ask for help in that matter. The more people with whom you share your expert knowledge, the more visible you become.

9 **Volunteer for high-priority projects.** You gain the greatest visibility by doing high-quality work on high-priority projects. Before you agree to join a planning committee, project team, or task force, ask yourself if this assignment will help advance your career by getting the attention of senior executives and other key contacts you'd like to make.

When you join an important project, consider being the one who summarizes and distributes the notes of your meetings to senior leadership. Presenting to senior leadership is a great way to make yourself visible.

10 Take an active role in your professional association. There are many benefits to joining and actively participating in your professional association. In addition to staying up to date with what is going on in your industry, you also develop leadership competencies that are outside your current experience at work. And from a self-promotion standpoint, you become better and more widely known in your industry.

See Figure 8.1 for a concise list of the 10 ways to boost your visibility.

 The more people know about you and the good work you do, the more visible you become and the greater impact you have.

Preparing Your Elevator Speech

Every encounter with someone from the C-suite is a chance to build or deplete your leadership presence. When a senior leader says "Tell me about yourself," how do you respond? If don't have a well-crafted and well-rehearsed elevator speech, you are missing one of the most powerful tools in your leadership presence tool kit.

Next time you attend a corporate event, make sure you come prepared with, ready to deliver at any moment, a clear, concise statement that points out what you do now but emphasizes what you want to do in the future and why you're qualified to do that. Senior leaders are assessing your level of

Figure 8.1   Ten Ways to Boost Your Visibility

VISIBILITY

① Add a photo to your email signature

② Speak up

③ Interact with executives

④ Work on a cross-functional team

⑤ Take advantage of your performance review

⑥ Know when to brag

⑦ Publicize your successes and those of your team

⑧ Position yourself as an expert

⑨ Volunteer for high-priority projects

⑩ Take an active role in your professional association

maturity, your ability to communicate, and how much command you have of your business. Being prepared with a short but effective elevator pitch gives you a huge advantage in terms of visibility and positioning.

One of my clients introduces himself this way: "I'm the manager of a project team that I've motivated and coached to get results that have exceeded all expectations. I'm looking for opportunities to use my skills to make an even bigger impact."

Another client memorized a list of updates that she can state clearly and succinctly. Her list includes an overview of her department, team successes, and how these successes help serve the goals of the company at large.

How about you?

What are three key points you'd like to make if you met one of your organization's executives and he/she said: "Tell me about yourself."

 You never know when or where you'll meet the executive who could skyrocket your career, so you should always be prepared.

Gaining Online Visibility

Social media sites geared for professionals, such as LinkedIn, are invaluable tools in helping you become visible to professionals outside of your organization. LinkedIn's members include executives from all Fortune 500 companies, so it is a great place to communicate your expertise and interests.

While less professionally focused, Twitter and Facebook are also helpful outlets for developing and managing your online presence.

Whichever site you choose, make sure your biography reflects how you want to be perceived and that it is complete with schools attended, places worked, and community groups you are involved with. You will also look more polished if the picture you post with your bio is a professional photograph.

Once you've created your online presence, invite people you already know to join you. "Follow" or "friend" them and check out their connections. If you see someone you don't know but would like to connect with, ask a friend to virtually introduce you. It's a good idea to share a noteworthy update on what you are working on at least once a week. You might mention something you're working on or an interesting item you've discovered. Be sure to engage others in the conversation by asking for their opinions or help and praise or recommend others in your online community.

Contribute articles and blog posts when you can. Make sure they are informative, well written, timely, and valuable to readers. You can also repost other people's articles and blogs that reflect your interests, expertise, and values.

Social media provides a platform to connect with people you would never have the opportunity to meet face-to-face.

Networking

When you think of networking, do you see yourself socializing with ease and grace—or does the very word "networking" increase your stress level and send shivers down your spine?

Social capital is the wealth (or benefit) that exists because of your social relationships. Your network is your social capital. It is the value you create by your connections to others. There is no more valuable commodity in today's business environment—and no more valuable skill—than becoming a master networker.

Social networks are especially important in knowledge-intensive sectors, where people use personal relationships to find information, do their jobs, and advance their careers.

Here are six strategies that will transform your networking experience from frightening to fun.

1 It's about building relationships. Many people hate to network because they think of networking as a function of sales. Although you can develop new business as a result of networking, the real objective is to make connections and build professional relationships. Master networkers know how to listen. The best networkers I know spend most of their time looking for some way to be of assistance to the other person. This could be as simple as a restaurant recommendation or an introduction to someone they would like to meet at an event.

If you have a great conversation with someone at a networking event and exchange contact information, send him or her a note afterward and mention something specific that made your conversation memorable. If you recommended a restaurant, send them a review of it. If you offered to send them an article or introduce them to someone not at the event, remember to follow through.

Next time you find yourself at a networking event, pretend that you are the host of the event and that your job is to help others have an enjoyable time. Approaching people with this attitude (and a genuine smile) immediately resonates in a highly positive way.

2 **Relax and be comfortable.** If you want people to see you as comfortable and friendly, you need to avoid creating barriers between you and other people. For example, if you head to the beverage and food stations to load up on refreshments as soon as you arrive, your glass and plate end up as physical barriers to networking. This makes you look closed off and resistant. By keeping your body free of barriers, you appear open and approachable.

And if you are asked about your career goals, I advise getting comfortable talking about where you are now and what you would like to achieve in the future. By letting others know where you are heading, you increase the likelihood of attracting a supporter or a valuable resource.

3 **Bring a buddy.** As the saying goes, there is safety (or at least support) in numbers. If you are an introvert or have a high level of anxiety when it comes to networking, ask if you can bring a guest. Simply having someone you know at the event can help alleviate networking angst and also provide an ally if you need to make an early exit.

You can attend the event together, and you can even approach a group together, but avoid staying with that person to the exclusion of meeting other people. It helps if your buddy has similar networking goals, so you can make sure that you are both having engaging conversations.

4 Connect by asking questions. It can be tough to walk up to a stranger and start a conversation, no matter how confident you are. That's why having an opening line ready to go is crucial. Good ice-breaking questions get the conversation started because they encourage others to talk. Questions like these can help open a conversation:

- o What brings you to this event?

- o How do you know the host?

- o Where have you come in from?

- o Did you have as much trouble getting here as I did?

- o What sort of work do you do?

If you are networking at a conference, you might ask: What presentation did you like best? What made that stand out?

5 Get to know people. People like to be asked about their aspirations, motivations, and passions. You can deepen conversations by asking what they like most about what they do, what's new in their industry, and what attracted them to that profession.

One of my favorite questions to ask is: "What is the most unusual thing you've done? Tell me something people would be surprised to know about you." Unless you've asked this before, you'll be surprised at all the wonderful, crazy, funny, and endearing stories you'll be told.

6 Find a way to stay connected. Gracefully ending a conversation leaves the other person feeling valued and appreciated. It's worth your time and effort to adopt your own version of one of these exit remarks.

- o Direct: "It was really nice meeting you. Do you have a card so I can have your contact information?"

o Indirect: "I've taken up enough of your time. You'll want to mingle and meet more people. Thank you so much for speaking with me."

o Connecting: "There is someone here I think you should meet. May I introduce you?"

o Excuse: "There is something (or someone) I need to check on. It's been a pleasure talking to you."

Figure 8.2 Enhance Your Networking

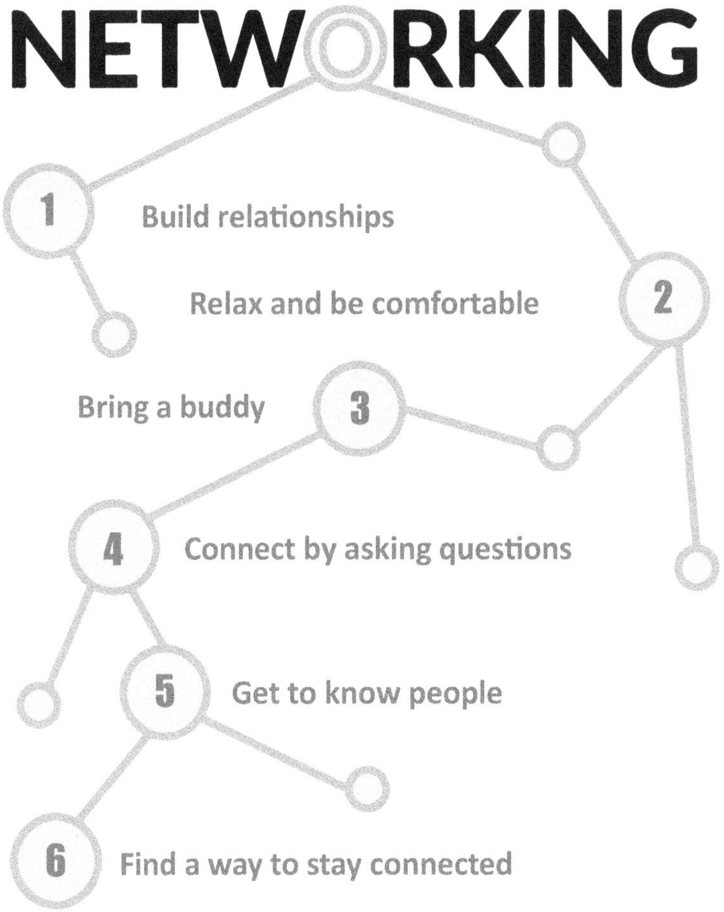

NETW RKING

1 Build relationships

Relax and be comfortable 2

Bring a buddy 3

4 Connect by asking questions

5 Get to know people

6 Find a way to stay connected

Meeting the right person at the right time can make a huge difference in your career—and you never know who may turn out to be the right person.

Mentors, Sponsors, and Role Models

Each of us, during our careers, needs help. Luckily, there are experienced and generous people who willingly give of their time and experience to help you learn from their experience and expand your network. Whether you work with a mentor, a sponsor, or a role model—or all three—you gain the benefit of learning from and gaining access to the network and influence of someone farther along in their career.

Mentors are people who support you and offer career advice. Hopefully, one of your mentors is your boss, as your boss is crucial for your success. To strengthen your relationship with your boss, you need to keep him/her consistently informed. When you complete a project successfully or placate an irate customer, send your manager a brief email outlining the result as soon as it happens. Of course, you need to get your facts straight and not exaggerate or stretch the truth. Think of this kind of self-promotion as less about bragging and more about keeping your manager up to date about the results of your work. Your achievements not only make you look good, but they reflect well on your boss.

My clients who have at least one mentor tell me they gain confidence, feel more comfortable speaking up, have access to a valued opinion when making career decisions, and gain insight into the organization's culture and unspoken rules.

The relationship between a mentor and mentee is often informal with you reaching out when you need input.

Sponsors go beyond giving advice and feedback. They are less talk and more action. Sponsors usually are senior leaders in your organization, and they are people who promote you to their peers. They introduce you to the "right" people in the organization and publicize your accomplishments and potential. You benefit and gain status in the organization because these influential people believe in you. Sponsors offer advice on your executive presence and pave the way for your leadership promotion. Sometimes sponsors will create an opportunity for you without you even knowing it.

Finding a sponsor typically happens in one of two ways:

1 A company's sponsorship program (Check with human resources to see if your organization offers one.)

2 Independent sponsorship, where you find one on your own by asking your boss or HR department for advice on possible candidates

In either case, you need to choose wisely by identifying successful individuals you like, respect, and trust. Then work on a project with them, talk to them at company events, or schedule a coffee or lunch to get to know them on a more personal basis.

When working with a mentor or sponsor, make sure you are doing your part.

- Be clear about what you want from each conversation: What are your needs? What are your challenges?
- Ask them about their career path—and lessons learned along the way.

- Take the opportunity to build your political savvy: What are the important trends? What projects and initiatives are coming up? What gets people noticed?
- Be enthusiastic, organized, focused, and reliable.
- Be receptive to feedback.
- Keep them posted on your progress.
- Give credit for helpful advice.
- Say thank you—often.
- Make the relationship reciprocal by actively looking for ways to be helpful to your mentor or sponsor. Don't wait to be asked.

Role models are people you observe and admire. You may not know them, but you study the way they conduct themselves, with whom they associate, how they dress, how they speak, and how they use body language to their advantage.

Think about a leader you admire and find ways to behave like the leader you want to be. The more you do it, the easier it becomes. When faced with a difficult decision, choose a role model you believe would handle the situation effectively. Ask yourself: "What choice would my role model make when faced with this decision?"

As talented and hardworking as you are, to get to the next level, you need people who support and actively promote you.

Mentors   Sponsors   Role Models

If you don't take the time to promote yourself, the next key assignment or promotion will go to whomever has gained the visibility and credibility that makes it easy for the decision maker think of him or her as the best candidate. I want that visible and credible candidate to be you.

To get ahead, you have to make people aware of your talents and abilities.

Key Takeaways

- If you don't create your own brand, other people will do it for you.

- The more people know about you and the good work you do, the more visible you become and the greater impact you have.

- You never know when or where you'll meet the executive who could skyrocket your career, so you should always be prepared.

- Social media provides a platform to connect with people you would never have the opportunity to meet face-to-face.

- Meeting the right person at the right time can make a huge difference in your career—and you never know who may turn out to be the right person.

- As talented and hardworking as you are, to get to the next level, you need people who support and actively promote you.

- To get ahead, you have to make people aware of your talents and abilities.

9

Leadership Presence for Women

Women face unique challenges when it comes to being perceived as leaders. One of them is the unconscious bias that results in fewer leadership opportunities being made available to women. Although few people today would say that women can't be great leaders, women hold only 18 percent of senior leadership positions among 2,300 organizations surveyed worldwide.[1] This is not because there are fewer women in the workforce or they are less qualified. Globally, women comprise almost half (48.5 percent) of the global workforce.[2] According to a recent study by Jack Zenger and Joseph Folkman, women are found to be 84 percent more effective than men in leadership competencies such as taking initiative, acting with resilience, practicing self-development, driving for results, and displaying high integrity and honesty.[3] Research also finds that women make teams smarter; "while there's little correlation between a group's collective intelligence and the IQs of its individual members, if a group includes more women, its collective intelligence rises."[4]

With all of the evidence that suggests that women are as capable if not more capable than men in leadership roles, it is still incredibly difficult to change the status quo. "Managers—male and female—continue to take viable female candidates out of the running, often on the assumption that the woman can't handle or don't want to do certain jobs due to family obligations. It's no wonder that, when researchers ask both men and women to draw a picture of a leader, they'll almost always draw a male figure."[5]

This implicit (unconscious) bias shows up in comments like:

- "I never thought a woman would be interested."
- "Can you get the coffee?"
- "We've never hired a woman for this position before."
- "We need someone who is going to be tough."
- "We would have invited you but didn't think you'd want to get a sitter."
- "I didn't think you'd want that much responsibility."

In this chapter, I'll uncover some of the other challenges that we women face, both externally and internally. I'll also provide tips for women seeking to overcome those challenges and optimize their strengths to increase their leadership presence.

The Double-Bind Paradox

He's the boss. You're bossy. He's successful and liked. You were better liked before you got promoted. That's the double-bind paradox.

As males rise in rank and status at work, they retain (and often increase) their perceived likability. Men can be both powerful and likable.[6] Unfortunately, the same is generally not true for women. Although women must project authority in order to advance in the business world, the more powerful they appear, the less they are liked.[7]

Blame it on the stereotype of women as nurturing, sensitive, and collaborative. When their behavior is congruent with these traits, women are liked but not seen as especially powerful. When their behavior runs counter to the stereotype, they are perceived negatively.[8] A frequently cited study, the Heidi/Howard case, shows that when the same highly assertive and successful leader is described to graduate students of both genders, that leader is seen as far more appealing when identified as a male rather than a female.[9]

There is a fundamental mismatch between the qualities traditionally associated with leadership and those traditionally associated with women.[10] When women disrupt gender stereotypes, they may be seen as competent leaders but disliked. When they soften their communication style to conform, they're often not seen as strong leaders.[11]

One study showed how women and men are described differently in performance reviews. It was found that words like "bossy," "abrasive," "strident," and "aggressive" are used to describe women's behaviors when they lead; words like "emotional" and "irrational" describe their behaviors when they object. All of these words show up at least twice in the women's reviews.[12] Among these words, only "aggressive" shows up in men's reviews at all.[13] It shows up three times, twice with an exhortation to be more aggressive.[14]

Stanford University communication professor Clifford Nass conducted research to see if students would apply gender stereotypes to computerized voices. In one study, half the subjects were tutored by computers with male voices and half by computers with female voices. When the material being taught was about love and relationships, students rated their female-voiced tutors as having more sophisticated knowledge of the subject than the male-voiced tutors. The female-voiced tutors were rated significantly less informative about technical subjects than the male tutors, even though both computers read the same information.[15]

In a *New York Times* interview, Dr. Nass said, "Our studies show that directions from a female voice are perceived as less accurate than those from a male voice, even when the voices are reading the exact same directions. Deepness helps, too. It implies size, height and authority. Deeper voices are more credible."[16]

As a woman, how do you navigate these shifting gender expectations, social roles, and leadership requirements? The most successful women I've worked with start by increasing their internal and external self-awareness. They are deeply aware of their personal values and boundaries while also maintaining a keen sense of how others perceive them. With this awareness, they can adapt and adjust their interactions to achieve the best outcome in a particular situation. Research at Stanford University Graduate School of Business also shows that women who are assertive and confident, but who can turn these traits on and off depending on the social circumstances, get more promotions than other women, or even than men.[17]

Recognize and nurture your ability to adapt to the style needed for the situation you are in.

Bridging the Confidence Gap

Sandra was introduced to me as a talented business professional with exceptional leadership skills. She was being
groomed for a top executive position and was looking for
some executive coaching. At the end of our first session, this
accomplished woman turned to me and said, "I want you to
know how nervous I was meeting you. I was afraid that you
wouldn't find me worthy to work with."[18]

This is a shocking statement coming from such an accomplished woman, and to be honest, it should have surprised
me. Unfortunately, it didn't, because I'd heard comments like
this before from other equally accomplished female clients.

In one study of 985,000 people from 48 countries, men and
women were asked to rate their self-esteem. The research
found men from all countries have higher self-esteem than
women and that the confidence gap was most evident in
highly developed countries like the United States.[19]

One of the reasons for this gap is that men and women respond differently to success. Part of this has to do with their
perceived locus of control. Because men tend to have a more
internal locus of control around achievements, they are more
likely to attribute success to personal factors (their ability,
talent, effort) and to minimize the impact of external forces
or factors.

Women, in contrast, tend to do the opposite. Women have a
more external locus of control when they succeed and are
more likely to attribute success to external factors, such as
good timing or luck, while at the same time they internalize
failure as a result of personal shortcomings. Because of a

lack of awareness of their true ability and potential, women are often less willing to take the risks needed to pursue opportunities. In fact, women rarely attempt something unless they feel 100 percent certain they can achieve it; men typically only have to feel 60 percent certain.

Oddly, this lower level of self-esteem is most prevalent in high-achieving, high-potential women who, in spite of their level of achievements, still have a tendency to be self-limiting. More often than not, women tend to hang back in discussions until they are fully confident in their answers, while men tend to leap forward with bold ideas even if they are not certain that they are correct. Low self-esteem and the resultant lack of confidence also are why women may ask for raises and promotions less often and with less assuredness than their male counterparts.

Women are also more likely to use tentative language, including tag questions ("That's okay, isn't it?"), qualifiers, and minimizers.[20]

And women apologize—a lot more than necessary. If you find yourself constantly apologizing, even for trivial things, break that habit.

Here are three tips to help you overcome your hesitation and share your ideas with full confidence in your ability.

1 **Prepare for meetings by knowing how valuable you are.** Many of the women I coach don't quite believe they belong at a senior leadership table. If that is the case for you, you may need to remind yourself that you are an asset to the organization and that your unique perspective is based on your hard-won expertise and experience. Start by answering these two questions:

o How do my experience, background, and insight contribute to and serve the discussion at hand?

o How do my overall efforts make a positive difference to the organization?

Remember, research finds if a group includes more women, its collective intelligence rises.[21]

Never go into a meeting doubting your own value.

2 Develop conscious competence. Competence bears little relationship to confidence. Only when you are aware of how good you are do you become more self-confident.[22]

Several years ago, I coached a woman to prepare for a job interview. I asked her to tell me what she did exceptionally well that she'd want a prospective employer to know. She was silent for several seconds. Finally she sighed and said, "I really don't know. I do a lot of things well, but when I do, I don't notice it."[23]

To build conscious competence, you need to notice and acknowledge your achievements. No one should be a bigger fan of you than you. When you do something well, ignore the urge to pass it off as really nothing and instead mentally acknowledge (and celebrate) your success.

Becoming aware of how skilled, smart, and talented you are is crucial to displaying leadership presence.

3 Stop waiting to be perfect. Nothing builds confidence like taking action, but perfectionism is a confidence killer that can lessen your willingness to take a professional risk.

Men are not shy at raising their hands for projects—or jobs—for which they are not fully qualified, but women often focus on their missing skills or gaps in expertise and, as a result, let good opportunities pass by.

It's important for everyone, especially women, to take chances and embrace risk in order to move forward in their careers, and it's very rare that one person possesses every single qualification for a new opportunity. Instead of waiting to be an exact fit for a challenge, step outside your comfort zone, believe in yourself, and trust your abilities.

Don't wait to be perfect and don't overanalyze every opportunity. Go for it!

Women with Low Confidence Are in Good Company

Every time I was called on in class, I was sure that I was about to embarrass myself. Every time I took a test, I was sure that it had gone badly. And every time I didn't embarrass myself—or even excelled—I believed that I had fooled everyone yet again. One day soon, the jig would be up.
—Sheryl Sandberg, Chief Operating Officer, Facebook

So I have to admit that today, even 12 years after graduation, I'm still insecure about my own worthiness. I have to remind myself today, *You are here for a reason.* Today, I feel much like I did when I came to Harvard Yard as a freshman in 1999 . . . I felt like there had been some mistake—that I wasn't smart enough to be in this company and that every time I opened my mouth I would have to prove I wasn't just a dumb actress.
—Natalie Portman's 2015 Harvard Commencement speech

> I have written 11 books but each time I think, uh-oh, they're going to find out now. I've run a game on everybody, and they're going to find me out.
> —Maya Angelou, Author and Poet

Figure 9.1   Bridging the Confidence Gap

Getting Emotional

I want to cry when I'm happy, when I'm sad, when I'm frustrated or overwhelmed or demoralized. Maybe you do too. Women shed more tears than men because we have higher levels of prolactin, the hormone that controls the development of tear glands.

Unfortunately, tears in the workplace lessen your credibility by making you appear weak and unable to maintain self-control. If you're leading a team, you need to project confidence and authority, so crying doesn't help. It is admirable to be emotionally connected to your work, but you are also responsible for delivering results. You can be invested in your role without having it bring you to tears.

If you do feel tears coming on, here are five suggestions for managing your emotions.

1 **Get angry.** Women have been told that expressing anger is not "ladylike," so we often resort to tears instead of risking a true display of anger. The next time you feel anger, don't let it turn into frustration and sorrow. Instead, let it strengthen your resolve to speak up, to politely disagree, and to assert your point of view.

2 **Get out.** If you are about to cry or if you actually begin to cry, excuse yourself and leave the room to find a private place to calm down. Continuing to cry in front of your boss or colleagues only makes a difficult situation worse.

3 **Explain your emotion.** "As you can see, I feel strongly about this" or "I get emotional about this because I care so much" or "I want you to know that I'm very worried about what happened, and as we discuss it I may get upset."

One new female leader made this announcement when she became visibly emotional addressing her department. "I want you to know this is part of my leadership style. I bring my emotions to work and I let you see exactly what I'm feeling. I think our organizational culture can benefit from this kind of emotional honesty."

4 Prepare for a worst-case scenario. Mentally rehearse how you want to handle a highly emotional situation. This mental preparation can give you a sense of control.

5 Break the cycle. The key to defusing any trigger event is taking the time needed to interrupt the trigger-reaction cycle. Try to recognize the first sign of emotional overload and then pause long enough to regain your composure. (Use the "Stop—Breathe—Affirm—Relabel—Respond" technique from Chapter 4.)

Get Angry	Get Out	Explain	Prepare	Break the Cycle

 Use emotion to underscore your passion and concerns, but stay in control.

Body Language Traps and Tips

You are naturally empathetic and likable. You smile a lot, nod to encourage others to continue speaking, and often tilt your head in the universal sign of giving someone your ear.[24] Great! You are displaying the warm body language that will continue to serve you well in building the kind of inclusive, collaborative environment that unlocks innovative potential of your team. So, don't stop sending these warm and very effective nonverbal cues.

At the same time, it's important to recognize that excessive or inappropriate displays of warm signals or coming across as overly polite can work against you by making you look less powerful and less competent.

Here are five body language traps that women typically fall into and tips for avoiding those traps.

Trap 1: Waiting Your Turn

In business meetings, men take control by talking more than women and interrupting more frequently.[25] Women are more likely to sit quietly and wait for their turn to speak.

Tip: Learn to Interrupt

Former U.S. Secretary of State Madeleine Albright shares, "Probably every woman you know, certainly every woman I know, has been in meetings where you're the only woman in the room, and you want to make some kind of a comment and you think, *Okay, I'm not going to say that, because it sounds stupid.* And then some man says it, and everybody thinks it's completely brilliant, and you're really mad at yourself for not having spoken. I had that experience most of my life."[26] The first piece of advice Albright has for up-and-coming women professionals is "Learn to interrupt."

Trap 2: Physically Condensing

Try this now: Sit in a chair with your legs tightly crossed, bring your elbows into your waist, and clasp your hands together and place them on your lap while slightly rounding your shoulders. It's not surprising that most people would evaluate that posture as powerless—but it may surprise you to know that some version of this very posture is the way most women sit. We tend to condense our bodies, keeping our elbows to our sides, tightly crossing our legs, and contracting our bodies to take up as little space as possible. And when we do, we don't look like leaders. We look physically smaller, weaker, and more fragile than we are.

Tip: Take Up Space

Remember that power and authority are nonverbally demonstrated by expanding into height and space. You look more authoritative when you stand tall by pulling your shoulders back, widening your stance, and holding your head high. When you sit, uncross your legs and put both feet flat on the ground, take up more space by placing your arms on the arms of your chair, and straighten your posture. You will instantly look surer of yourself.

Trap 3: Smiling Excessively

Women are more likely to cover negative feelings with a smile, which is one reason we smile more than men. But excessive or inappropriate smiling can be confusing and can lessen your credibility, especially when you're discussing a sensitive subject, stating an objection, or giving negative feedback.

Tip: Know When to Look Serious

Employed at the right times, such as during an initial meeting with a potential business client, smiling can be one of your most powerful and positive nonverbal cues. It can help you appear friendly and likable. But when the subject turns serious, you need to drop the smile and look serious.

Trap 4: Nodding Too Much

When a man nods, it means he agrees. When a woman nods, it means she agrees—or is listening to, empathizing with, or encouraging the speaker to continue.[27]

Tip: Know When to Keep Your Head Still

Constant head nodding can express encouragement and engagement, but it can also limit your ability to project authority and power. Nodding is helpful when you want someone to expand on their thoughts, but when you are stating your opinion with authority, keep your head still.

Trap 5: Speaking in a Girly Tone of Voice

Recently I've been to several business meetings where I heard women using a soft, singsong tone of voice, speaking in a breathy way, and sounding like little girls. By using a girlish tone of voice, those leaders are less likely to be perceived as having the gravitas necessary to command respect or advance their careers.

Tip: Cultivate an Authoritative Voice

The sound of your voice matters twice as much as what you're talking about. If you want people to think "I hear her speak and I believe her," then it is worth the effort of cultivating an authoritative voice. You can do this without sounding harsh or overbearing.

Make sure you are speaking clearly and loudly enough to be heard, letting your breath support rather than obscure your words. Remember that nothing kills credibility faster than letting your voice rise at the end of a sentence. When making a declarative statement, use the authoritative arc, in which your voice starts on one note, rises in pitch through the sentence, and drops back down at the end.[28] (It can help to think to yourself the word "period" as you end the sentence.)

Keep using your warm body language but add power and authority signals in situations where you are called to lead.

Figure 9.2   Body Language Traps

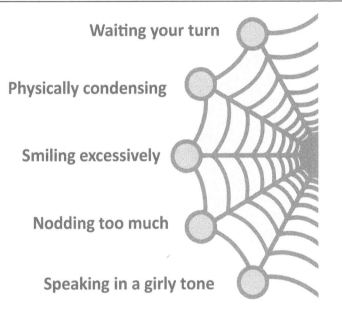

Waiting your turn

Physically condensing

Smiling excessively

Nodding too much

Speaking in a girly tone

Dress for Success

The old saying "You can't judge a book by its cover" may be true, but packaging designers around the world have created an industry betting that people *do* judge products based on how they look. And career counselors still advise their clients to dress for the job they want, not the job they currently have.

The question "How should I dress at work?" comes up at every women's conference I address. My answer? There is no one "right" look. The appropriate way to dress is determined by your company culture, the impression you want to make, and what you are comfortable wearing.

Culture

There are many different types of workplaces, ranging from open creative offices to more traditional corporate environments. Your corporate culture may embrace a smart, sophisticated look, or it may favor a more funky or trendy look. Your employer may even have a written dress code with examples of the types of clothing that are and are not acceptable in that workplace.

Circumstances

Since clothing is part of your nonverbal communication, appropriate dress is also a way of expressing respect for the situation and the people in it. Your clothing makes an impression, but the impression you want to make will depend on the circumstances. You might "dress up" by wearing a suit or dress if you have a job interview, if you are asking for a promotion, or if you have a big workplace event, such as an important meeting or presentation. A savvy female's look may change depending on her audience. I know a woman in the human resources department of a Silicon Valley company who has two sets of clothing in her office.

She puts on one when she's dealing with techies and another when she is meeting with executives.

I also know a management consultant who wears stiletto heels with hot pink, turquoise, and fire-engine red silk dresses at work in her New York City office. But when she meets with a conservative client or one going through a difficult time, she transforms into a prim professional whose outfit matches the way she wants to be perceived. In her words, "The success I dress for is that of my client."

Comfort

Wearing clothing that feels inauthentic will lessen someone's self-confidence, so women should dress in a fashion that makes them feel comfortable. I also advise women to take themselves and their professional reputation seriously. When I talk about dressing for success with women in or aspiring to a leadership role, I mean dressing in ways that build, not diminish, their credibility as professionals. The balance lies in finding a look that is both comfortable and appropriate for the impression you want to make.

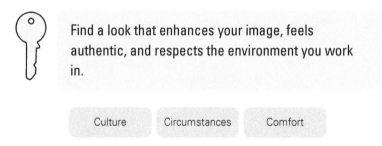

Find a look that enhances your image, feels authentic, and respects the environment you work in.

Culture   Circumstances   Comfort

Here are some general dos and don'ts to keep in mind.

- **Do** make sure your clothes fit properly, which may mean updating your wardrobe if you've changed sizes.

- **Don't** let your appearance take the focus away from what you have to say.

- **Do** keep it classic. Trendy clothes are fun, but classics look professional. That said, you also want to keep your wardrobe updated by adding one or two items that reflect the current style.

- **Don't** wear alluring or skimpy clothing. It may be attention-getting to do so, but women who wear low-cut tops and too-short/too-tight skirts are viewed as less intelligent.

- **Do** dress up when giving a presentation to senior management. Consider wearing a jacket. It's a nonverbal sign of authority and power.

- **Don't** get sloppy. If you look sloppy, people will assume that your work is also sloppy. Instead, think "polished and professional." Cleanliness and neatness always send a positive message, and never more so than in a professional environment.

- **Do** observe the successful women in senior positions in your organization and take cues from how they dress.

- **Don't** forget that the office party is a work-related event that is just as important as any other business function. Wear your festive and attractive attire but keep it tasteful.

- **Do** stay physically fit. Regardless of your size, your clothes will look best on your toned and fit body.

 Your appearance should never distract from your presence, credibility, and performance.

Bring Your Femininity to Work

In the musical comedy *My Fair Lady*, Professor Higgins sings this lament: "Why can't a woman be more like a man?" When I give a leadership presence program especially for women leaders, I get asked a similar question: "Why do I have to change my feminine leadership style to be more like a man?"

My response to seminar attendees is to ask this question: "Why do you think that maintaining good posture, directly stating a point of view, and taking well-calculated career risks is masculine? I think it's highly feminine, and I think you should bring your femininity—all of it—to work."

You reveal your truest self by embracing your femininity. Femininity is about the ability to be vulnerable, patient, and understanding. It's about finding out what people's strengths are and leveraging them to benefit everyone in the business. It's about connecting, encouraging, and supporting your team members and allowing them to bring their full, authentic selves to work. This kind of leadership is lacking in most businesses, and management teams are starving for it.

Next I list the feminine leadership skills that are the most valued. As you read this list, check off all the behaviors you already display. These are the very skills needed for the kind of leadership that is fast becoming a requisite for organizational success.

Feminine Leadership Skills

- Feminine leaders share power.
- Feminine leaders share credit.
- Feminine leaders have confidence in the decision-making ability of their teams.
- Feminine leaders are good delegators.
- Feminine leaders make sure everyone on the team has a voice.
- Feminine leaders share information.
- Feminine leaders are good listeners.
- Feminine leaders don't command and control, they influence and include.
- Feminine leaders use empathy to connect with others.
- Feminine leaders pick up crucial cues by reading body language.
- Feminine leaders use warm body language to encourage participation.
- Feminine leaders use their intuition to supplement their business acumen.
- Feminine leaders stand up for their teams.
- Feminine leaders help others grow and develop.
- Feminine leaders see the big picture.
- Feminine leaders build trust-based relationships.
- Feminine leaders create psychological safety.
- Feminine leaders understand how emotions influence decisions.

Feminine leaders display warmth and empathy while also projecting power, authority, and confidence.

When you look at the requirements for displaying leadership presence, there are areas where women have a tremendous advantage—and one area where we fall behind. Every female leader I have ever coached lacked confidence. Without a doubt, if there's one thing you can do to build your leadership presence, it's to look for the inner strength to become a full participant in whatever leadership team you belong to. Believe in yourself, take more risks, don't stay quiet, and don't let yourself be sidelined.

In that spirit, here's a story I heard from a business leader in London: "It is harder for women to get noticed, I believe, simply because they tend to be more collegiate and polite. In Graham Green's novel *Our Man in Havana*, the character of Beatrice makes her appearance when she shoots her soda siphon at Captain Segura, thus making him leave the party. She explains she did it so she would always be remembered as the woman who emptied soda over the trousers of the most powerful man in town. If you want to stand out, sometimes you have to be a Beatrice."

Key Takeaways

- Recognize and nurture your ability to adapt to the style needed for the situation you are in.

- Never go into a meeting doubting your own value.

- Don't wait to be perfect and don't overanalyze every opportunity. Go for it!

- Use emotion to underscore your passion and concerns, but stay in control.

- Keep using your warm body language but add power and authority signals in situations where you are called to lead.

- Your appearance should never distract from your presence, credibility, and performance.

- Feminine leaders display warmth and empathy while also projecting power, authority, and confidence.

10

Cross-Cultural Leadership Presence

I have worked (given speeches or seminars) in 28 countries, and I have traveled to a dozen more. More important, I have access to an international network of business leaders who graciously shared their insights and experiences about global leadership presence for this chapter. What I've discovered is that regardless of culture or country, the broad description of a leader with presence is essentially the same: someone who is calm, not manic; who is passionate, but keeps their passions under control; someone who is emotional, but in a deliberate and constructive way; someone who is confident but not arrogant; someone who shows empathy and compassion but not subservience; and someone who has a strong personal vision but also values other people's opinions and points of view.

This, however, doesn't mean there aren't differences in how leadership presence is displayed in various cultures. Each culture has its own rules about proper leadership behavior. When working across cultures, your leadership presence is enhanced by your ability to understand the established values, beliefs, norms, perceptions, and behaviors learned and practiced by that culture.

Let's consider eye contact. In the United States, the United Kingdom, and most European cultures including Spain, France, and Germany, making eye contact is seen not only as appropriate but as necessary for establishing leadership presence. In Australia, eye contact signals openness and respect. In India, empathetic eye contact generates trust. In Brazil, it signals confidence. In Middle Eastern cultures, glancing away from a speaker shows a lack of interest.

However, there are also cultures where making eye contact may be impolite or even considered as an act of aggression. In China, for example, it's considered downright impolite to look straight into another person's eyes. In many South American, African, and Asian cultures, avoiding eye contact (or at least limiting it) with a superior is a show of respect, while extended eye contact is a sign of disrespect or even aggression.

From culture to culture, the norms differ regarding whether you should make eye contact or not, whether you should be direct or talk around an issue, whether you should be reserved or enthusiastic. As my friend and cross-cultural expert Stuart Friedman often reminds me, "In general, leadership presence is shown by a strong adherence to the values that are held in the highest regard in that particular culture, country, and company."

In this chapter, I provide a multicultural perspective of leadership presence so that you will be able to more accurately anticipate how your leadership style is likely to be perceived when working across cultures. I'll explore the difference between "high-" and "low-context" cultures, reserved and effusive cultures, formal and informal cultures, and cultures that relate to time as a commodity or a constant. I'll offer insights for communicating nonverbally across cultures, and you'll discover how three universal leadership qualities—confidence, credibility, and connection—are displayed internationally.

It is important to keep in mind that I am providing examples from a relatively small sample and that cultural stereotypes are valid only for the clues they provide regarding what to expect in general. Nothing in this chapter should be taken as definitive, and none of my observations are meant to suggest that everyone you meet from a culture or country will act identically. Different regions in the same country may have unique business styles. For example, in the United States, New York, San Francisco, and Atlanta have their own regional views about leadership presence. In Europe, southern Germany is very different from northern Germany (Catholic South vs. Protestant North, etc.)—and East Germany, which used to be part of the Eastern Bloc, has its own special history. Remember, too, that you don't have to share or agree with cultural differences, but you will need to avoid an "I'm right; you're wrong" attitude. Most important, remember that you can't view the behavior of others totally free of your own cultural bias—which is, after all, exactly how others are evaluating you.

High-Context vs. Low-Context Cultures

Cultural anthropologist Edward T. Hall created a system of classification, called "proxemics," that identifies cultures by the general style in which they communicate.[1] Low-context cultures (LCCs) communicate predominantly through verbal statements and the written word. Low-context communication is explicit, direct, and precise, with little reliance on the unstated or implied, which is why LCCs want details to be written in business contracts and why their verbal agree-ments are crafted more precisely. In high-context cultures (HCCs), communication depends more on sensitivity to non-verbal behaviors (body language, proximity, and the use of pauses) and environmental cues, such as the relationship of the participants, what has occurred in the past, who is in attendance, and the time and place of the communication. Rather than paying attention primarily to what is said, HCCs are alert for innuendo through tone of voice and subtle signals transmitted through eye contact, facial expressions, and silences.

From high- to low-context, here's how various cultures rank:

Figure 10.1   High-Context vs. Low-Context Cultures

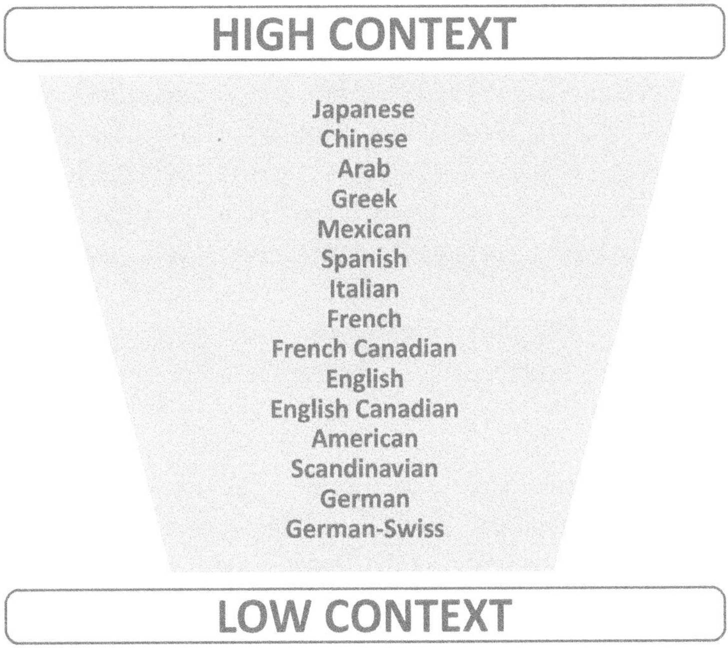

HIGH CONTEXT

Japanese
Chinese
Arab
Greek
Mexican
Spanish
Italian
French
French Canadian
English
English Canadian
American
Scandinavian
German
German-Swiss

LOW CONTEXT

At business meetings in LCCs, what is said and written down is most important. In HCCs, people look for meaning in silences, vocal tone, body language, and facial expressions.

Transactional vs. Interpersonal Cultures

Transactional and interpersonal cultures are on a spectrum similar to low- and high-context cultures: Transactional cultures, including the United States, Canada, Australia, and much of northern Europe, tend to focus more on getting down to work. Interpersonal cultures, including China, the United Arab Emirates, Mexico, and southern Europe, look primarily to build a relationship. Don't be surprised if a business meeting in Brazil starts by members talking about families, friends, and personal lives. Only after this exchange is it appropriate to discuss business. Likewise, in the Middle East, expect the first few minutes of a meeting to be dominated by a similar kind of personal conversation as it is considered rude to immediately jump into a business conversation. This personal-relationship-building aspect is so important in HCCs that leaders who approach business first without showing concern for personal matters usually fail.

When facilitating a global team meeting, leaders from transactional cultures gain presence by taking the extra time to get to know their interpersonal culture counterparts. In turn, those from more interpersonal cultures might also want to get to the point of the meeting more quickly if they are presenting to a large group from a transactional culture. The point, of course, isn't to abandon your cultural preferences but to increase cross-cultural effectiveness.

 In interpersonal cultures, building relationships is pivotal to displaying presence, while transactional cultures prefer getting down to work.

Reserved vs. Effusive Cultures

Different cultures display emotions differently. In some cultures, it is appropriate and even expected to get very emotional when debating an issue. In these effusive cultures, leaders tend to be more expressive and animated and to use larger and more frequent gestures. Examples of effusive cultures include the Arabs, Italians, Indians, and Latin Americans —which are all HCCs. But emotional displays can also be a part of LCCs. In Germany, for example, a normal negotiation may begin with a verbal attack so the speaker can gauge your reaction. If you are cowed, Germans tend to dismiss you. If you respond with confident and powerful body language, you will be respected.

As you might expect, emotion is an integral part of leadership presence in Mexico. It is common for leaders to show emotion with a bit of humor to defuse tension. The Chinese can also get emotional in business meetings since laughing, talking loudly, or yelling is not considered rude.

Yet even in cultures where emotional expression is common, there is a high regard for those who don't let emotions run wild. In Brazil, a leader's ability to control, rather than display, emotion is highly regarded. One Argentinian client I spoke with said, "Passion is so common in our culture that we take it for granted. But if I interact with a leader who is passionate, but also calm and precise, I know I'm dealing with a skilled professional."

Business leaders from reserved cultures, like Japan and the Scandinavian countries tend to tend to mask their feelings by keeping their emotional displays in check. In the United Kingdom, where coolness and aloofness are valued, jokes are preferred to raw emotion. Laughter is allowed, while shouting is an admission of defeat, and tears are a source of major embarrassment. Likewise, Australians prefer business dealings to be emotionally neutral.

In reserved cultures, displays of anger, distress, or excessive emotion can be perceived as career-limiting behaviors. Consider the case of an American-born Japanese IT manager who requested a relocation to work at his company's Tokyo office. Excited about the possibility, he flew to Japan and interviewed with the local team. His request was turned down. The reason? He was "too enthusiastic." Not a surprising response when you consider that most Japanese leaders adhere to the traditional ideal of a strong, silent, stoicism.

To show leadership presence in effusive cultures, communicate with passion and energy. In reserved cultures, it is wise to curb your enthusiasm.

Formal vs. Informal Cultures

The formality or informality of cultures is less dependent on whether it's an HCC or an LCC and more dependent on the historical and political background of a country. In informal cultures like the United States, Canada, Australia, New Zealand, Denmark, Norway, and Iceland, people believe that inequality of social status or class should be minimized. In the Netherlands, the egalitarianism of Dutch society is reflected in its business organizations. Executives do not usually display their power because the boss is considered part of the group. The managing director and employees are all considered coworkers, and people ignore authority when they deem it necessary.

In more formal cultures including many European and Asian nations, the Arab world, the Mediterranean region, and Latin America, people are more likely to be treated with greater or lesser deference according to their social status, family background, connections, education, and titles. French and Spanish business leaders, for example, tend to be autocratic, paternalistic, and sometimes militaristic. In fact, *cadre,* the French word for "manager," is borrowed from the armed forces.

People from informal cultures may regard their formal counterparts as distant, stuffy, or pompous while people from formal cultures often find informality to be insulting. If you are meeting with people in a formal culture and you call them "pal" or "buddy" or by their first name on first acquaintance, you are undermining your leadership presence. As one of my Malaysian clients explained with polite understatement, "We consider it rude and disrespectful to assume an intimacy that doesn't yet exist."

Your leadership presence will be evaluated more highly if you adjust your business etiquette and communication style (including the way you dress) to reflect the formality or informality of the culture you're dealing with.

Time as Commodity or Constant

Do you arrive on time for a business meeting? That may depend on whether you come from an LCC and view time as a commodity or an HCC, which thinks of time as more of a constant flow.

In the United States, we think of time as a sequential, linear commodity to "spend," "take," "use," "save," or "waste." This, naturally, makes arriving on time for a meeting important. The British are similar. If a meeting is to start at 2 pm, anyone joining 15 minutes late is considered rude. In Australia, arriving later than 10 minutes late is considered bad manners. In Germany, if a meeting is set for 2:00 to 4:00 pm, people will arrive at 1:50 pm and expect to leave promptly at 4:00.

Other cultures, including Italians, Arabs, and Chinese, view time as a constant force that cannot be contained or controlled. If you attend a business meeting in almost any South American country, don't be surprised or annoyed if people show up 30 minutes late. Also don't be surprised if a scheduled appointment in Kuwait isn't kept. Arabs feel no personal control over time. Instead, a favorite expression, *"Bukra insha Allah,"* which means "tomorrow if God wills," reflects their perceived inability to control time.

Here's another example. A female executive from South America was invited to a cocktail party in San Francisco, California. The hours on the invitation were stated as 5 pm to 9 pm. This was almost inconceivable to the executive. "How can anyone know when the party will be over?" she asked. To her way of thinking, a party can't be "timed." It begins when it begins and ends when it ends. I heard a similar viewpoint from a Brazilian businessman: "Our meetings have a time to start, but never to finish."[2]

 Depending on whether you think of time as a commodity or a constant, you will have an entirely different view of being on time for a business meeting.

Tips for Cross-Cultural Communication

Cross-cultural communication is challenging enough without having to worry about people getting lost in the middle of a conversation, so remember that for many of your international partners, English is a second (or third, fourth, or fifth) language. Here are a few of the more common verbal communication mishaps: humor, slang, jargon, metaphor, and abbreviations.

Humor

"Did you hear the one about the Scotsman who . . . ?" Well, if you did, keep it to yourself. Humor directed at yourself can have a positive effect, but only locals can make fun of their government, highway, neighbors, and themselves. There are few things you might do that are more offensive than making a joke at the expense of your host country.

Slang

- "Run that by me again."
- "Throwing the baby out with the bathwater."
- "It will never fly."

You may know exactly what these mean, but for many of your international colleagues, they are just confusing or meaningless expressions.

Jargon

- "Devil's advocate"
- "Dog and pony show"
- "Buy-in"

Jargon is a barrier to clear communication and shows a lack of cultural awareness.

Metaphor

- "Monday morning quarterbacking"
- "Waiting for the other shoe to fall"
- "That idea struck out"

Leaders in the United States are particularly fond of using sports metaphors in business presentations. It's easy to forget that almost all metaphors are culturally meaningful only where we learned them.

Abbreviations

- R&D
- P&L
- CEO

Transnational communicators realize that initialisms and abbreviations are most likely meaningless in other cultures.

 You display cross-cultural leadership presence when you speak simply and clearly.

Communicating Nonverbally across Cultures

Many nonverbal signals cross cultural lines. In fact, body language that is controlled by the limbic brain (like the freeze/fight/flight response to threat, blushing when embarrassed, lip compression when we don't want to respond, and the need to self-pacify when under stress) can be seen around the world. Facial expressions are also among the most universal forms of body language. The expressions used to convey fear, anger, sadness, and happiness are similar worldwide.[3] Here is how you can identify them:

- **Joy:** The muscles of the cheeks raise, eyes narrow, lines appear at the corners of the eyes, the corners of the mouth turn up.

- **Surprise:** The eyebrows raise and there is a slight raising of upper eyelids and dropping of the lower jaw.

- **Sadness:** The eyelids droop as the inner corners of the brows raise and (in extreme sorrow) draw together, and the corners of the lips pull down.

- **Anger:** The eyebrows pull together and lower, the lower eyelids tense, the eyes glare, and the lips tighten, appearing thinner.

- **Fear:** The eyebrows draw together and raise, the upper eyelids raise, the lower eyelids tense, and the lips stretch horizontally.

- **Disgust:** The nose wrinkles, the upper lip raises, and the corners of the mouth turn down.

- **Contempt:** The only unilateral expression. The cheek muscles on one side of the face contract and one corner of the mouth turns up.

However, not all nonverbal cues are universal. In the high-stakes world of international business, nonverbal communication often speaks for itself. Unfortunately, much of the meaning may be lost in translation. The most innocuous of gestures, when its intent is misinterpreted, can wreak havoc on your leadership presence. Think of how confusing it might be in Bulgaria, for example, where a nod is "no" and a head shake means "yes."

Even the simplest hand movement can get you into cross-cultural trouble—and that starts with how you wave hello and good-bye. Our common North American wave, with the hand moving side to side, means "no" throughout Mediterranean Europe and Latin America. In Peru, that gesture means "come here." In Greece, that same gesture is a serious insult, and the closer the hand to the other person's face, the more threatening it is considered to be.[4] Here are six more emblematic hand gestures that differ from culture to culture:

- The thumbs-up gesture that North Americans and members of many other cultures flash to signify "Well done!" is considered offensive in certain locales (Australia is one) and should be avoided.

- Rotating the palm up and curling your finger is a common gesture we use in the United States to ask someone to come closer. But this gesture is used only to beckon dogs in many Asian countries; it is considered extremely rude in China, East Asia, Singapore, and Malaysia.

- Flashing the "V" sign for victory in the United States suggests business negotiations have been successful, but that signal will be rude and offensive in the United Kingdom, Australia, and New Zealand, especially if the back of the hand is facing out.

- The "good luck!" crossed-fingers gesture that we use in the United States has several other meanings. In Turkey, for example, the gesture is used to break a friendship. Elsewhere it is used to indicate that something is good, to swear an oath, or as a symbol for copulation.

- If you want to indicate the you are alert in France, Germany, and Turkey, you might signal with an eyelid pull, in which the forefinger is placed on the cheekbone and pulled down to widen the eye a little. In Spain and Italy, that signal says "stay alert"; in Austria it signals boredom, and in Saudi Arabia it indicates stupidity.

- Pointing your index finger at someone or something is rarely a good idea, even in the United States. It is considered especially rude in China, Japan, Indonesia, and Latin America. In Europe, you'll simply look impolite, but in many African countries, it is considered a deep insult if you point at someone because the index finger is used only for pointing at objects—never at people.

Greetings also differ:

- Although a handshake is the business greeting gesture most common around the world, even that has its cultural nuances. In England, the handshake comes with three to five hand pumps, while in Germany or France, one or two pumps is considered sufficient. In Asia, the grip is much lighter, and you can insult a Latin American by withdrawing your hand too quickly.

- Exceptions to the handshake greeting may be seen in Japan and South Korea (bowing), in India (the *namaste*—palms held together in a prayer gesture), and in Arabic and Islamic cultures, where handshakes between men and women are not always viewed as appropriate.

- Some cultures prefer to greet with a kiss on the cheek. Scandinavians give a single kiss, the French prefer a double, and the Dutch, Belgians, and Arabs go for a triple kiss.

Cultural sensitivity to nonverbal communication plays a large part in building rapport with your global business partners.

Checklist for International Business Meetings

Although the international business arena may blur distinctions between some cultures, it hasn't eliminated them completely. Even representatives from different parts of the European Community still encounter—and stumble over—differences in cultural style. When the prototypical reserved British businessperson confronts the machismo of the Latins or interacts with the argumentative French, there is still potential for cultural clash. And no region of the world has greater variety and diversity of languages, races, and religions than Asia, although the cultures of the countries of Asia and the Pacific have crisscrossed and intermingled for centuries. There is still much cultural variance in the world.

The following list is the minimum information that I try to know about a host country before I travel there to give a business presentation.

Greeting Behaviors

How do businesspeople greet one another?

- Do they kiss, bow, or shake hands? If they shake, do they prefer a firm or a gentle grip?
- When should business cards be exchanged? How should cards be handled?
- How are introductions made?
- What is considered good manners for greeting senior executives when they enter a room?
- How are you expected to address others?

An American business leader traveled nine thousand miles to meet clients in Singapore. On the trip over, he memorized the names of all the key men he was to see. The board chairman was Lo Win Hao, and the American began his greeting by addressing him as Mr. Hao, only to be told by a colleague that he had been too friendly and informal much too soon. In Chinese, the surname comes first and the given name last. It was as if he was calling his clients Mr. Bob or Mr. John.

Business Protocol

- How important is it to be prompt for a business meeting?
- What is the protocol for seating around the conference table?
- How much space between people in normal business situations is their comfort zone?
- How much time should be spent in pleasantries and social interaction?
- Who takes the initiative in getting down to business?
- When is the use of humor appropriate?
- What topics of conversation are considered inappropriate or unprofessional?
- How much physical contact is appropriate?
- What is appropriate behavior when leaving and saying good-bye?
- How are males and females expected to interact in business situations?

A woman traveling in the Middle East as chief emissary for her Fortune 500 corporation was surprised after meeting with men all day to be placed at a separate table with their wives at dinner.

Social Behavior

- How much socializing is not only expected but necessary for doing your job successfully?

- What are the important holidays, and how are they observed?

- What is the normal meal schedule? Is there a daytime rest period?

- Is it typical to be invited to a private home for dinner? If so, how are you expected to reciprocate? If you are invited for dinner, should you arrive early, on time, or late? If late, how late?

- Are dinner or lunch meetings most desirable?

- Does one drink or not at a business meal? Are you expected to offer a formal toast before drinking?

- What is the proper seating order at a restaurant or dinner table?

- Are females and/or spouses included in after-hours business entertainment?

- What are considered good table manners?

- Is it expected practice to exchange gifts? If so, what kinds of gifts are proper, and how should they be presented?

- What kind of compliments are expected, and which are inappropriate?

I received this email from an executive when he first arrived in Saudi Arabia: "What do you do when you've been asked to dinner by your Muslim host and (in the middle of the meal) he takes out his prayer rug to pray? Well, they hadn't covered that in my pre-assignment training, so I was bewildered . . . do I stop eating, bow my head, what? Luckily, I was not the only guest, so I followed the lead of others, who quietly continued talking and eating until our host returned to the dinner party."

In addition to the preparations just listed, I suggest doing some background reading on the host country—its history, national heroes, fine arts, native sports, and political, social, and economic structure. I also suggest having your business card, brochures, and handouts translated into the host country's primary language.

Prepare for cross-cultural business dealings by finding out all you can about the country and culture you'll be working in.

Leadership Presence Qualities across Cultures

What I find most interesting about considering leadership presence across cultures is not our differences but our similarities. Next I present some typical responses to a short questionnaire I ask audience members to fill out when I speak at global events.

Question 1: How do leaders display confidence?

United Kingdom

- "The bad ones often go with 'machismo' and other traits of toxic power-driven body language, cutting people off midsentence and generally not really listening, putting people and their efforts down. The good leaders display confidence with calm and composure that suggest both strength and integrity."

- "They have a deep knowledge of the subject being discussed. They listen to people with genuine attention, never hesitating to praise and give credit to people and their ideas and efforts."

- "They acknowledge and take responsibility for their own mistakes and empower their teams to make things happen."

United Arab Emirates

His Highness Sheikh Zayed bin Sultan Al Nahyan was the president of UAE for over 30 years. His leadership is evidenced in the following advice: "The Ruler should not have any barrier which separates him from his people."[5]

Other responses include:

- "Leaders show confidence by highlighting their knowledge, contacts, and achievements."
- "They act decisively and give direction."

South America

- "Leaders show confidence by being emotionally emphatic and calm yet able to make a strong stand when needed."

- "In my culture, leaders display confidence by communicating with excellence, maintaining eye contact, and demonstrating an ability to stay calm."

India

- "Leaders display confidence through their grasp on contextual data—a display of information-driven conviction."
- "They show passion and investment in the topic through their tone of voice, body language, and choice of words."
- "Confident leaders are comfortable on stage. They take time, walk around while presenting, have a solid stance when they stand, and make eye contact with the audience."
- "They use touch—especially in one-on-one conversations—to instill confidence in the listener."

Question 2: What communication skills does a leader need to be seen as credible?

United Kingdom

- "Clarity of purpose in sharing their message, calm and rationality under pressure, ability to demonstrate empathy by listening, and finding the connection (and hopefully synergy) between what the team wants and what the leader is trying to achieve."
- "Courteous—no matter what status their interlocutor."
- "Taking their time to explain their point of view"
- "Demonstrate the ability to see both sides to a question"
- "Good listening skills, positive body language, inclusive language."

- "Interpersonal, presentation, trustworthy and trusting (openness and aligned to the 'why'), ability to inspire confidence and commitment, plus storytelling that relates, energizes, and resonates."

United Arab Emirates

- "Leaders increase their credibility through active listening."
- "They give and receive constructive feedback."
- "They show empathy and responsiveness."

South America

- "While many aspects like a powerful and inspiring oratory might help, we tend to analyze our leaders not by what they say but by what they do."
- "If I interact with a leader for the first time, I'd be checking to see if the leader looks at my eyes when shaking hands and if his body language is correct. If so, those might indicate to me he is a good leader."
- "Credible leaders give straight answers to questions and are not afraid to say 'I don't know'."

India

- "Leaders are the most credible when they are concise and can present complex information with simplicity."
- "They are clear in giving directions and setting expectations."
- "They provide an inspiring vision of the bigger picture and the value of the team's work within that vision."
- "Credible leaders let people know that they are accessible and available for a conversation on the topic."

- "Sometimes in India, position and titles play a great role in building credibility."

Question 3: How important is it for a leader to show connection through displaying empathy?

United Kingdom

- "Empathy is all important and needs to be evident. We will gladly follow people whom we trust to have our concerns and ambitions in mind."

- "Empathy should always be displayed in the context of understanding individual's needs. It is important to demonstrate alignment with, awareness of, and commitment to others."

- "When leaders display genuine empathy, it adds to the authenticity we should be bringing to work on a daily basis."

United Arab Emirates

- "On a scale from 1 to 10 it is an 8."

- "Empathy begins by understanding the emotions of team or individuals and responding properly to these feelings."

South America

- "Empathy can be very important to successful leadership because, in my culture, a leader with low empathy can be ignored or sabotaged, even if he/she is absolutely right about their ideas."

- "As the Latin Americans are passionate, empathy is very important for us. Empathy is displayed by ensuring that all procedures, roadmaps, or decisions consider how other people feel. An example of empathy would be for me to cancel a one-on-one meeting because my coworker is having a bad time; instead, inviting him for coffee so we can talk about it."

India

- "The game-changing difference between a manager and a leader is neither their ability to see the big picture nor to exceed expectations with business outcomes, but rather their ability to work with different sets of people. That takes empathy."

- "In an age where knowledge and expertise are being commoditized by digital media, empathy is the new age differentiator in leadership."

- "Empathy and the 'personal touch' are much appreciated and build trust and loyalty."

- "It's very important for leaders to convey genuine caring for the well-being of the people in their teams. Not only personal well-being but career advancement paths and encouragement. However, it should not be displayed through excess informality. It's more the empathy and support of an elder toward a junior: encouraging the development of others through supervision, appreciative feedback, and mentoring."

- "Active listening, paraphrasing to make people feel understood, reading between the lines, and hearing what is unsaid are all parts of displaying empathy—and some of the keys to succeed in business today."

Question 4: What is your advice for mid-level leaders heading for senior leadership positions?

Universal Tips

- Stay flexible and ready to adapt rapidly to new challenges.
- Stay aligned and informed about your organization's goals.
- Adopt a growth mindset.
- Focus on delivery with and through people, which takes empathy and understanding.
- Coach and develop other strong and capable professionals.
- Lead with authenticity—be yourself but go beyond being egocentric.
- Embrace differences and value diversity.
- Lead for results by focusing on what matters and collaborating with purpose.
- Display your leadership ability by running a best-in-class, high-performing team that constantly exceeds expectations for customers.
- Contribute positively to the senior leadership team.
- Build your own brand.
- Ensure balance in all for everyone, including yourself!

 Many qualities of leadership presence are perceived positively across cultures.

Cross-cultural leadership presence has its cultural variations, but I think you will find there are more similarities than differences. People around the world respond to leaders who inspire and motivate them, who are knowledgeable, who unify a team around a common purpose, who display compassion and generosity, and who create environments of psychological safety.

Although part of your cross-cultural leadership presence is given by your position or title, the larger portion is how you present yourself and is reflected in how you dress, how you enter a room, how you express your key points, how well you handle pressure, and how effectively you connect with other people. In essence, cross-cultural leadership presence basically relies on the same foundation as it does within your own culture—the ability to align other people's impressions of you with your best authentic self.

Key Takeaways

- At business meetings in LCCs, what is said and written down is most important. In HCCs, people look for meaning in silences, vocal tone, body language, and facial expressions.

- In interpersonal cultures, building relationships is pivotal to displaying presence, while transactional cultures prefer getting down to work.

- To show leadership presence in effusive cultures, communicate with passion and energy. In reserved cultures, it is wise to curb your enthusiasm.

- Your leadership presence will be evaluated more highly if you adjust your business etiquette and communication style (including the way you dress) to reflect the formality or informality of the culture you're dealing with.

- Depending on whether you think of time as a commodity or a constant, you will have an entirely different view of being on time for a business meeting.

- Cultural sensitivity to nonverbal communication plays a large part in building rapport with your global business partners.

- You display cross-cultural leadership presence when you speak simply and clearly.

- Prepare for cross-cultural business dealings by finding out all you can about the country and culture you'll be working in.

- Many qualities of leadership presence are perceived positively across cultures.

Conclusion

Leading in Times of Uncertainty and Change

Leaders are facing greater uncertainty and change than ever before, and adjusting to a post-pandemic workplace only adds to the disruption. Consider the circumstances facing leaders and their organizations today:

- Rapidly changing technologies make yesterday's choices obsolete.

- Budgets are tightened when the economy is unpredictable, leaving employees with fewer resources.

- Your company relies on a shifting stream of alliances. A competitor today may be your business partner tomorrow—and sometimes both at the same time.

- Companies are restructuring on a yearly basis.

- Mergers and acquisitions are on the rise.

- Customers are demanding "better, faster, cheaper" everything.

- New competitors arise seemingly from out of nowhere.

- The pace of change is accelerating.

- Employees are increasingly skeptical about committing to business strategies and are experiencing transformation fatigue from continuous organizational change efforts.

Yet this is our reality, and leadership success belongs to those who can keep a workforce positive, resilient, and engaged while dealing with the tsunami of change that is turning our organizations upside down.

As a leader, you need to understand that dealing with change is highly emotional for your workforce. Transformation is both unpredictable (responding to unforeseen circumstances) and unnerving (requiring employees and businesses to reinvent themselves while they are at the top of their game). Your best employees may become discouraged as they realize that they cannot rely on the tried-and-true techniques that have served them well in the past. Success will require continuous learning and adaptation.

To help your organization (or department or team) manage the difficulties of change, you need to inspire and motivate them with a powerful vision of the future. A compelling vision provides employees with meaning and allows them to put into context the challenges they facing in dealing with change. As a leader, your ability to engage and inspire your workforce is dependent on whether you can relate to their emotions and create a compelling story that both captivates their imaginations and motivates them to work with you toward that shared vision.

In times of organizational uncertainty, people instinctively look to their leaders in order to get a better sense of how to interpret and react to a situation. How you as a leader react has an effect on your employees. In times of stress, employees look to you to help them understand how to respond to challenging situations.

Some leaders make the mistake of thinking that they need to protect their employees. Under this rationale, they present change with a too-positive spin. This is a mistake. Your team knows when you are not being authentic so any attempt to sugarcoat the truth is bound to backfire and lead to greater distrust.

In addition to providing a positive spin, many leaders make things worse by communicating change only through traditional communication vehicles—speeches, newsletters, videos, intranets, email, and the like. Although leaders can talk about change in speeches and newsletters, what motivates and inspires people to change is what their leaders actually do. Your employees are looking to you to model the way.

Managing through massive change and disruption is the ultimate test of your leadership presence, requiring you to be your most credible and composed self. Your employees are paying particular attention to your ability to be both *credible* and *composed*—what you say and how you say it.

In times of change, your employees need you to be authentic. This means that you share information openly and honestly even when it's not advantageous for you to do so. It means being transparent and sharing everything from financial information to business opportunities. It requires providing your employees with the necessary information about competitive and industry trends so that they can understand how their actions impact the business.

In addition, you need to recognize that how you act and where you show up matters. Are you spending all of your time in meetings with your senior leadership team? Are you fostering a hierarchy where only top executives solve problems, make decisions, and set the change agenda? Instead of fostering creative and innovate solutions, this outdated command-and-control approach results in an overburdened senior management team and a workforce that feels distrusted and powerless in the face of change.

To be competitive, a company needs to draw on all of its assets—its people, the quality of the information that people possess, and the ability to share that knowledge with others in the organization. When companies make strategy development a participatory event, the entire organization benefits. Employees feel empowered and motivated to help, and the organizational strategies that result are stronger, resulting from the collective wisdom, experience, and creativity of the organization.

Do you make it a point to regularly check in and have all-hands meetings so that your employees feel acknowledged and informed about challenges and potential solutions? When your messages are not followed up with direct action, your words can disintegrate into empty slogans.[1] A communication strategy that is not aligned with the actions of leaders is useless.

When you do communicate with your organization, how you express emotion, the faces you make, the way you stand—all of these signals are subject to interpretation and given meaning by those around you. In particular, people are very responsive to facial gestures and the perceived emotions underlying them. We humans frequently imitate gestures that we see and the emotions underlying them. That is why when someone smiles at you, you feel compelled to smile back; when someone frowns, you can feel your mood start to shift.

The effect of people's expressed emotional state on others was the focus of an interesting study at Yale School of Management.[2] A business simulation experiment gave two groups of people the assignment of deciding how much of a bonus to give each employee from a set fund of money. Each person in the group was to get as large a bonus as possible for certain employees while being fair to the entire employee population.[3] What the people in each group didn't know was that an actor had been secretly assigned to each group.

In the first group, the actor was negative and downbeat. As a result, that group experienced conflicting agendas that led to stress and tension among all group members. In the second group, the actor was positive and upbeat. Everyone in that group ended up feeling good about the result. The finding: The emotional tone of the meetings followed the lead of each actor, although none of the group members understood why his or her feelings had shifted.[4]

We're hardwired to mimic expressions and emotions and have been doing so since infancy. When we see a picture of a happy face, we automatically smile. Looking at a photograph of an expression can lead us not only to mirror the expression but the underlying emotion as well. Each of us gives and responds to hundreds of facial expressions daily—from colleagues' grins to clenched-jaw displays around the conference table. Looked at another way, as a leader, you are part of an emotional chain-reaction effect. Part of establishing and maintaining your leadership presence is to lead others to be part of the positive emotion solution—and not part of the problem.

Leadership Presence in the Next Generation of Leaders

In addition to the massive uncertainty and change in our organizations, we are also experiencing changes in our homes and families. Technology is changing not only our lives but also our brains. Although this is true for everyone, it is most relevant for children—those "digital natives" who were born into a world of computers, smartphones, text messaging, tweeting, and video games. And did you know that while the brain is developing circuitry for social networking, neural circuits for one-on-one personal communication are beginning to atrophy?

When we rewire our brains for technology, we don't use or strengthen the neural pathways used for human interaction. As a result, we stop learning how to respond to people and how to accurately read their nonverbal cues. We also become less empathetic.

A study by the University of Michigan found that the empathy levels of college students have been declining over the past 30 years, with the steepest drop in the last 10 years.[5]

Here are four tips to help your children develop the body language and empathy necessary to be leaders of tomorrow:

1 **Limit your own screen time.** Before you think about limiting the screen time of your children, ask yourself: "What kind of example am I setting?" Do you text while driving or bring your smartphone to the dinner table? Your children may seem to ignore everything you say, but they take many of their behavior cues from watching what you do.

2 **Dine together.** I know it's difficult when you and your children have conflicting and overlapping schedules, but it's around the dinner table that kids learn to socialize, empathize, and pay attention to important nonverbal cues.

3 **Talk to your children about their body language.** Let your children know that you are reading their body language every day and that you can tell from their posture and facial expressions if they are having a great or a not-so-great day. Also let them know that their nonverbal signals—shoulder shrugs, eye rolls, eye contact, smiles, and the like—are being read and reacted to by their teachers, coaches, and friends.

4 **Use empathetic listening and warm body language.** Many of the same principles of empathetic listening and warm body language signals that apply to leadership are equally applicable to parenting:

o **Give your undivided attention.** When having an important conversation with your children, sit so you'll be at the same height, turn your entire torso toward whomever is speaking, put your smart phone away, and focus solely on them.

o **Smile, lean slightly forward, and keep your body posture open** (no crossed arms, please) to encourage a child to tell you more.

o **Subtly mirror** their posture, gestures, facial expressions, and tone of voice to show your child that you understand.

o **Use your empathetic listening skills.** Ask questions to help you fully understand their point of view. And don't rush in with a solution to every problem. Make sure your children are asking for it before you offer to help.

Success has often been compared to an iceberg. We see only the 10 percent tip of the iceberg, the achievement. We see the Nobel Prize winner, the Olympic champion, the entrepreneur who became a billionaire. What we don't see is the

90 percent that is hidden beneath the surface. We don't see the effort, the sacrifices, the dedication, the tenacity, and the plain hard work that is the foundation of everyone's success—whether they are scientists, athletes, or business professionals.

As a successful leader, you have already worked hard, made sacrifices, and persevered—and you realize that continually developing your leadership skills is a career-long undertaking.

The process of aligning people's perception of you with your true talent and potential so that you stand out as the leader you are will also take time, grit, determination, and an ever-deepening faith in yourself. But I guarantee you, you can do it—and, as I have seen with my coaching clients and seminar participants, it will be well worth the effort!

Let Me Support You

If you have questions, comments, or success stories to share, I'd love to hear from you. You can reach me by email: Carol@CarolKinseyGoman.com.

NOTES

Chapter 1

1 Carol Kinsey Goman, "Leadership Presence: Sending All the Right Signals," IMS, https://ims-online.com/faculty/Dr.-Carol-Kinsey-Goman/390 (archived at https://perma.cc/D95V-PU5D)

2 Carol Kinsey Goman, "Do You Look Like a Leader?," *BBN Times*, April 7, 2018, www.bbntimes.com/companies/do-you-look-like-a-leader (archived at https://perma.cc/54UW-GRG5)

3 Carol Kinsey Goman, "10 Questions to Power Up Your Leadership Presence," *Insights*, July 13, 2016, https://insights.newscred.com/power-up-your-leadership-presence (archived at https://perma.cc/CH8Y-NN2Q)

4 Carol Kinsey Goman, Speeches and Seminars, 2020, https://carolkinseygoman.com/speeches-and-seminars (archived at https://perma.cc/3DKX-YSLA)

5 *2016 Women in Sales Awards*, www.slideshare.net/ZarsMedia/women-in-sales-awards-europe-2016-magazine (archived at https://perma.cc/3GB6-TRD6)

6 Ibid.

7 Carol Kinsey Goman, "10 Body Language Traps for Women in the Workplace," Troy Media, July 8, 2019, https://troymedia.com/career-human-resource-information/body-language-traps-women-work (archived at https://perma.cc/MB64-G499)

8 Meredith Lepore, "8 Body Language Mistakes to Avoid," TheLadders.Com (archived at https://perma.cc/G384-6GGQ), November 21, 2019, www.theladders.com/career-advice/

8-body-language-mistakes-you-need-to-avoid (archived at https://perma.cc/NZ7V-EVUC)

9 Carol Kinsey Goman, "How Your Body Language Can Defeat the Double-Bind Paradox," August 24, 2017, www.women-in-technology.com/wintec-blog/how-your-body-language-can-defeat-the-double-bind-paradox (archived at https://perma.cc/8QAS-JTSV)

10 Carol Kinsey Goman, "8 Body Language Tips for Video Meetings," Zoom Blog, September 17, 2013, https://blog.zoom.us/wordpress/2013/09/17/8-body-language-tips-video-meetings (archived at https://perma.cc/4S39-2SXC)

11 Carol Kinsey Goman, "Body Language of Listeners," Global Listening Center, 2019, www.globallisteningcentre.org/body-language-of-listeners (archived at https://perma.cc/X6CS-AUWG)

12 Ibid.

13 Jeff Grabmeier, "Share Your Goals—but Be Careful Whom You Tell," *Ohio State News*, September 3, 2019, https://news.osu.edu/share-your-goals--but-be-careful-whom-you-tell/ (archived at https://perma.cc/2YMD-9S2T)

14 Howard J. Klein, Robert B. Lount Jr., Hee Man Park, and Bryce J. Linford, "When Goals Are Known: The Effects of Audience Relative Status on Goal Commitment and Performance," *Journal of Applied Psychology 105*, 4 (2020): 372–389. https://doi.org/10.1037/apl0000441 (archived at https://perma.cc/EY2M-4Q4Y)

15 A. J. Adams, "Seeing Is Believing: The Power of Visualization," December 3, 2009, *Psychology Today*, www.psychologytoday.com/us/blog/flourish/200912/seeing-is-believing-the-power-visualization (archived at https://perma.cc/VBT4-5WXQ)

16 Lien P. Pham and Shelley E. Taylor, "From Thought to Action: Effects of Process- versus Outcome-Based Mental Simulations on Performance," *Personality and Social Psychology Bulletin*, February 1, 1999, doi.org.10.1177/0146167299025002010

Chapter 2

1 Carol Goman, "Do You Look Like a Leader?," *Vunela*, n.d., www.vunela.com/do-you-look-like-a-leader (archived at https://perma.cc/6J7G-TLLR)
2 www.wrike.com (archived at https://perma.cc/4ZE9-9DJZ)
3 Carol Kinsey Goman, "Virtual Body Language," ExecuNet, July 10, 2014, www.execunet.com/virtual-body-language (archived at https://perma.cc/MG2P-Z6JE)
4 Carol Kinsey Goman, "Has Technology Killed Face-to-Face Communication?," TheLadders.com, November 28, 2018, www.theladders.com/career-advice/has-technology-killed-face-to-face-communication (archived at https://perma.cc/QF4Y-2V3C)

Chapter 3

1 Carol Kinsey Goman, "Don't Try to Fake Confidence— Do This Instead," TheLadders.com, April 18, 2018, www.theladders.com/career-advice/dont-try-to-fake-confidence-do-this-instead (archived at https://perma.cc/MKA9-MHWT)
2 Carol Kinsey Goman, "10 Body Language Myths that Can Limit Your Success," TheLadders.com, March 21, 2018, www.theladders.com/career-advice/10-body-language-myths-limit-success (archived at https://perma.cc/GK6T-ZK2R)
3 Carol Kinsey Goman, "How Women Can Escape the Impostor Syndrome Trap," BBN Times, March 7, 2018, www.bbntimes.com/companies/how-women-can-escape-the-imposter-syndrome-trap (archived at https://perma.cc/W38L-QG54)
4 Ibid.
5 A. Pascual-Leone, D. Nguyet, L. Cohen, J. Brasil-Neto, A. Cammarota, and M. Hallet, "Modulation of Muscle

Responses Evoked by Transcranial Magnetic Stimulation during the Acquisition of New Fine Motor Skills," *Journal of Neurophysiology* 74, vol. 3 (1995): 1037–1045, www.ncbi. nlm.nih.gov/pubmed/7500130 (archived at https://perma.cc/ BE94-9VSJ)

6 Goman, "Don't Try to Fake Confidence."

7 M. Lefkowitz, R. R. Blake, and J. S. Mouton, "Status Factors in Pedestrian Violation of Traffic Signals," *Journal of Abnormal and Social Psychology* 51, No. 3 (1955): 704–706, doi.org/10.1037/h0042000

8 Carol Kinsey Goman, "Body Language Secrets of Successful Negotiation," American Management Association, January 24, 2019, www.amanet.org/articles/body-language-secrets-of-successful-negotiation (archived at https://perma.cc/TV8Y-DQBV)

9 Ibid.

10 Ibid.

Chapter 4

1 Workplace Bullying Institute, "Results of the 2010 WBI U.S. Workplace Bullying Survey," www.workplacebullying.org/ wbiresearch/2010-wbi-national-survey/ (archived at https://perma.cc/4PXQ-SS8A)

2 J. P. Jamieson, M. K. Nock, and W. B. Mendes, "Mind Over Matter: Reappraising Arousal Improves Cardiovascular and Cognitive Responses to Stress," *Journal of Experimental Psychology: General* 141, no. 3 (2012): 417-422, DOI: 10.1037/a0025719

3 Carol Whipple, "Connecting Laughter, Humor and Good Health," University of Kentucky College of Agriculture, Food and Environment, May 2008, revised January 2018, HSW-CAW.807, www2.ca.uky.edu/hes/fcs/factshts/hsw-caw-807.pdf (archived at https://perma.cc/4H7P-ATJM)

4   S. Nejati, S. R. Esfahani, S. Rahmani, G. Afrookhteh, and S. Hoveida, "The Effect of Group Mindfulness-based Stress Reduction and Consciousness Yoga Program on Quality of Life and Fatigue Severity in Patients with MS," *Journal of Caring Sciences* 5, no. 4 (2015): 325–335, doi.org/10.15171/jcs.2016.034

5   Carol Kinsey Goman, "Having Trouble Dealing with Change? Get a Life!," American Management Association, January 24, 2019, www.amanet.org/articles/having-trouble-dealing-with-change-get-a-life- (archived at https://perma.cc/UQ3Y-24GQ)

6   Brock Armstrong, "How Exercise Affects Your Brain," *Scientific American,* December 26, 2018, www.scientificamerican.com/article/how-exercise-affects-your-brain/ (archived at https://perma.cc/27TZ-SYE9)

7   Kerri-Ann Jennings, "11 Best Foods to Boost Your Brain and Memory," *Healthline*, May 9, 2017, www.healthline.com/nutrition/11-brain-foods (archived at https://perma.cc/XV2K-RR9H)

8   Sarah Kivel, "How Sleep Primes the Brain for Emotional Intelligence," Key Step Media, October 22, 2018, www.keystepmedia.com/sleep-brain-kivel/ (archived at https://perma.cc/QKX3-PB7Y)

Chapter 5

1   Cigna, "New Cigna Study Reveals Loneliness at Epidemic Levels in America," May 1, 2018, www.prnewswire.com/news-releases/new-cigna-study-reveals-loneliness-at-epidemic-levels-in-america-300639747.html (archived at https://perma.cc/R6LN-BW5D)

2   Health Resources & Services Administration,"The 'Loneliness Epidemic,'" January 17, 2019, www.hrsa.gov/enews/past-issues/2019/january-17/loneliness-epidemic?utm_campaign=enews20190117&utm_medium=email&utm_

source=govdelivery (archived at https://perma.cc/52AG-733X)

3   N. I. Eisenberger, M. D. Lieberman, and K.D. Williams, "Does Rejection Hurt? An fMRI Study of Social Exclusion," *Science,* October 10, 2003, 290–292, DOI: 10.1126/science.1089134

4   Gabriel Doyle, Amir Goldberg, Sameer B. Srivastava, and Michael C. Frank, "Alignment at Work: Using Language to Distinguish the Internalization and Self-Regulation Components of Cultural Fit in Organizations," *Proceedings of the 55th Annual Meeting of the Association for Computational Linguistics,* July 30–August 4, 2017, pp. 603–612, www.aclweb.org/anthology/P17-1056.pdf (archived at https://perma.cc/VTT7-2BKW)

5   Carol Kinsey Goman, "3 Crucial Skills for Leading without Authority," TheLadders.com, June 20, 2018, www.theladders.com/career-advice/3-crucial-skills-for-leading-without-authority (archived at https://perma.cc/EG9L-TDYU)

6   William A. Gentry, Todd J. Weber, and Golnaz Sadri, "Empathy in the Workplace: A Tool for Effective Leadership," Center for Creative Leadership White Paper, 2016, www.ccl.org/wp-content/uploads/2015/04/EmpathyInTheWorkplace.pdf (archived at https://perma.cc/5X2Y-VQRG)

7   J. Sterling Livingston, "Pygmalion in Management," *Harvard Business Review* (January 2003), https://hbr.org/2003/01/pygmalion-in-management (archived at https://perma.cc/L4D9-6S2J)

8   Ibid.

9   Charles Duhigg, "What Google Learned from Its Quest to Build the Perfect Team," *New York Times Magazine,* February 25, 2016, www.nytimes.com/2016/02/28/magazine/what-google-learned-from-its-quest-to-build-the-perfect-team.html (archived at https://perma.cc/CL3P-WXPG)

10 Businessolver, 2019 State of Workplace Empathy, www.businessolver.com/resources/businessolver-empathy-monitor (archived at https://perma.cc/BWX5-7W9T)

11 "What's the Number 1 Leadership Skill for Overall Success,"
    DDI Media Room, February 23, 2016, www.ddiworld.com/
    global-offices/united-states/press-room/what-is-the-1-
    leadership-skill-for-overall-success (archived at https://perma.cc/
    LZR4-VWMS)
12 Westside Toastmasters, *Dimensions of Body Language,*
    Chapter 11: Common Gestures Seen Regularly, nd,
     https://westsidetoastmasters.com/resources/book_of_body_
    language/chap11.html (archived at https://perma.cc/R3CK-
    UYPT)

Chapter 6

1 Carol Kinsey Goman, "How Leaders Project Charisma,"
   June 27, 2018, TheLadders.com, www.theladders.com/
   career-advice/how-leaders-project-charisma (archived at
   https://perma.cc/UYR5-MH7A)
2 Carol Kinsey Goman, "The Body Language of Charisma,"
   LinkedIn, February 28, 2018, www.linkedin.com/pulse/
   body-language-charisma-carol-kinsey-goman-ph-d-
   (archived at https://perma.cc/68XZ-TWBQ)
3 Carol Kinsey Goman, "Managing Continuous Change,"
   American Management Association, January 24, 2019,
   www.amanet.org/articles/managing-continuous-change
   (archived at https://perma.cc/D85C-CEX7)
4 Ibid.
5 Ibid.
6 Patrick Allan, "How to be More Charismatic," *Lifehacker*,
   November 27, 2019, www.lifehacker.com.au/2019/11/
   how-to-develop-your-charisma-and-become-more-likable
   (archived at https://perma.cc/VZ6B-7UH2)
7 Carol Kinsey Goman, "A-to-Z Strategies for Building
   Collaboration," TroyMedia, February 21, 2020,
   https://troymedia.com/business/advice-for-entrepreneur-small-

business/strategies-building-collaboration (archived at
https://perma.cc/AGT3-RJ4G)

8 Ibid.

9 Ibid.

10 Bejoy Mathew, "The Secret Sauce of Successful Leadership:
Know the 5 D's of Leadership," December 13, 2015,
www.slideshare.net/BejoyMathew1/the-secret-sauce-of-
successful-leadership-know-the-5-ds-of-leadership
(archived at https://perma.cc/5EUR-JRKS)

Chapter 7

1 Carol Kinsey Goman, "10 Questions to Power-Up Your
'Leadership Presence,'" *First Republic*, www.firstrepublic.
com/articles-insights/life-money/build-your-business/10-
questions-to-power-up-your-leadership-presence (archived at
https://perma.cc/W3BZ-A6XL)

2 Ibid.

3 Ibid.

4 A. Pentland, *Honest Signals: How They Shape Our World*
(Cambridge, MA: MIT Press, 2008).

5 T. Tsukiura and R. Cabeza, "Orbitofrontal and Hippocampal
Contributions to Memory for Face-Name Associations: The
Rewarding Power of a Smile," *Neuropsychologia* 46, no. 9
(2008): 2310–2319, ncbi.nlm.nih.gov/pmc/articles/
PMC2517599 (archived at https://perma.cc/EN6A-WDPT)

6 Katrijn Steenbeke, "How Body Language Effects [*sic*] What
We Send Across," *marbl*, nd, https://marbl.be/inspiration/
how-body-language-effects-what-we-send-across (archived at
https://perma.cc/T837-QMNW)

7 Carol Kinsey Goman, "Five Mistakes People Make Reading
Body Language—and Five Nonverbal Signals That Send
Positive Messages," www.dilenschneider.com/files/Dilen_
FiveMistakes_31680_web.pdf (archived at https://perma.cc/
5P7M-A4VF)

8   Carol Kinsey Goman, "Body Language That Tells Your Team How You Really Feel," TheLadders.com, April 25, 2018, www.theladders.com/career-advice/body-language-that-tells-your-team-how-you-really-feel (archived at https://perma.cc/4DR3-5GSS)

9   Carol Kinsey Goman, "6 Powerful Ways to Make a Positive First Impression," TroyMedia, January 27, 2018, https://troymedia.com/business/advice-for-entrepreneur-small-business/6-ways-make-positive-first-impression (archived at https://perma.cc/ZP26-PJUQ)

10 Carol Kinsey Goman, "10 Body Language Tips to Power Up Your Career," TroyMedia, July 21, 2019, https://troymedia.com/career-human-resource-information/body-language-career-tips (archived at https://perma.cc/WC8H-8RRP)

11 Rachel Lefkowitz, "How to Be a Collaborative and Influential Leader (Using Body Language), Linkedin Learning Blog, November 4, 2019, https://learning.linkedin.com/blog/learning-tips/how-to-be-a-collaborative-and-influential-leader--using-body-lan (archived at https://perma.cc/RZ3C-BDJX)

12 www.commpro.biz/5-body-language-hacks-that-make-you-look-like-a-leader (archived at https://perma.cc/7RVH-MWEQ)

13 Duke Fuqua School of Business, "New Research Finds There May Be a 'Million Dollar Voice' for CEOs," April 17, 2013, www.fuqua.duke.edu/duke-fuqua-insights/ceo-million-dollar-voice (archived at https://perma.cc/XW9S-EMY6)

14 Carol Kinsey Goman, "10 Body Language Tips to Power Up Your Career," TroyMedia, July 21, 2019, troymedia.com/career-human-resource-information/body-language-career-tips (archived at https://perma.cc/9MW7-HA7U)

15 Wikipedia contributors, "Proxemics," *Wikipedia, The Free Encyclopedia,* https://en.wikipedia.org/w/index.php?title=Proxemics&oldid=934770665 (archived at https://perma.cc/3GCR-FDXM)

16 Ibid.

17 "Peter Drucker," *toolshero,* nd, www.toolshero.com/toolsheroes/peter-drucker/ (archived at https://perma.cc/UC9Y-FE52)

18 Carol Kinsey Goman, "New Year's Resolution: Sharpen Your Lie-Detection," *commpro*, nd, www.commpro.biz/new-years-resolution-never-to-be-lied-to-again (archived at https://perma.cc/9U4A-HXEZ)

19 Carol Kinsey Goman, "How to Read Body Language Like a Pro," TroyMedia, October 21, 2019, troymedia.com/career-human-resource-information/body-language-career-tips (archived at https://perma.cc/9MW7-HA7U)

20 University of Buffalo, "Can a Machine Tell When You're Lying? Research Suggests the Answer Is 'Yes,'" press release, March 26, 2012, www.buffalo.edu/news/13302 (archived at https://perma.cc/NR9T-XVF5)

21 Carol Kinsey Goman, "How to Spot a Liar at Work," TheLadders.com, May 9, 2018, www.theladders.com/career-advice/seven-ways-to-spot-a-liar-in-the-workplace (archived at https://perma.cc/GH4H-T2Q3)

22 Carol Kinsey Goman, "How to Spot a Liar at Work," American Management Association, January 24, 2019, www.amanet.org/articles/how-to-spot-a-liar-at-work (archived at https://perma.cc/P7SN-NAL4)

23 Ibid.

24 Carol Kinsey Goman, "How to Spot a Liar," *BusinessKnowHow*, June 5, 2018, www.businessknowhow.com/manage/spotliar.htm (archived at https://perma.cc/BGU7-DGWG)

25 David DeSteno, Cynthia Breazeal, Robert H. Frank, David Pizarro, Jolie Baumann, Leah Dickens, and Jin Joo Lee, "Detecting the Trustworthiness of Novel Partners in Economic Exchange," *Psychological Science* 23, no. 12 (2012): 1549-1556, doi: 10.1177/0956797612448793

26 Goman, "New Year's Resolution."

27 "How to Spot a Liar at Work," CMCAcorner.com, December 27, 2018, https://cmcacorner.com/2018/12 (archived at https://perma.cc/J3BF-UU6H)

28 Ibid.

29 Ibid.

30 A. Mehrabian, *Silent Messages: Implicit Communication of Emotions and Attitudes* (Belmont, CA: Wadsworth, 1981), www.kaaj.com/psych/smorder.html (archived at https://perma.cc/5H2L-ZDZ8)

31 Carol Kinsey Goman, "10 Body Language Myths That Limit Success," ExecuNet, January 9, 2018, www.execunet.com/10-body-language-myths-limit-success (archived at https://perma.cc/8GA7-2G4W)

Chapter 8

1 Shelley J. Correll and Lori Mackenzie, "To Succeed in Tech, Women Need More Visibility," *Harvard Business Review,* September 13, 2016, hbr.org/2016/09/to-succeed-in-tech-women-need-more-visibility (archived at https://perma.cc/59ME-BGNA)

Chapter 9

1 Michelle Peluso, Carolyn Heller Baird, and Lynn Kesterson-Townes, "Women, Leadership, and the Priority Paradox," IBM, nd, www.ibm.com/thought-leadership/institute-business-value/report/womeninleadership (archived at https://perma.cc/28UG-39SE)

2 Catalyst, "Women in the Workforce—Global: Quick Take," January 30, 2020, www.catalyst.org/research/women-in-the-workforce-global/ (archived at https://perma.cc/QDU9-958T)

3 Jack Zenger and Joseph Folkman, "Research: Women Score Higher Than Men in Most Leadership Skills," *Harvard Business Review,* June 25, 2019, https://hbr.org/2019/06/research-women-score-higher-than-men-in-most-leadership-skills (archived at https://perma.cc/8AF3-E548)

4 Anita Woolley and Thomas W. Malone, "Defend Your Research: What Makes a Team Smarter? More Women," https://hbr.org/2011/06/defend-your-research-what-makes-a-team-smarter-more-women (archived at https://perma.cc/759E-ES5C)

5 Heather Murphy, "Picture a Leader. Is She a Woman?," *New York Times*, March 16, 2018, www.nytimes.com/2018/03/16/health/women-leadership-workplace.html (archived at https://perma.cc/2GU7-5EZG)

6 Carol Kinsey Goman, "Tips for Women Heading to the Executive Suite," TheLadders.com, July 18, 2018, www.theladders.com/career-advice/tips-for-women-heading-to-the-executive-suite (archived at https://perma.cc/UP5V-NR7K)

7 Ibid.

8 Ibid.

9 Maria Katsarou, "Women & the Leadership Labyrinth: Howard vs. Heidi," Leadership Psychology Institute, May 28, 2017, www.leadershippsychologyinstitute.com/women-the-leadership-labyrinth-howard-vs-heidi/ (archived at https://perma.cc/9JHY-YY2K); Carol Kinsey Goman, "Figure of Speech," *Comstock's Magazine*, March 1, 2014, www.comstocksmag.com/article/figure-speech (archived at https://perma.cc/A9G5-KRCT)

10 Katsarou, "Women & the Leadership Labyrinth."

11 Gwen Moran, "Women Still Feel They Have to Soften Their Communication at Work," *Fast Company*, October 11, 2019, www.fastcompany.com/90413951/women-still-feel-they-have-to-soften-their-communication-at-work (archived at https://perma.cc/4DYL-43W8)

12 Siham Nurhussein, "Gendered Code Words: Recent Study Examines the 'Abrasiveness Trap,'" *Shattering the Ceiling*, September 9, 2014, www.shatteringtheceiling.com/gendered-code-words-recent-study-examines-the-abrasiveness-trap (archived at https://perma.cc/4YDD-5CT7)

13 Jane C. Woods, "Which Word Is Used to Describe Women But Not Men?," Life Labs, December 9, 2015, https://lifelabs.psychologies.co.uk/users/997-jane-c-woods/posts/4067-

which-word-is-used-to-describe-women-but-not-men (archived at https://perma.cc/TNL5-E2GJ)

14 Kieran Snyder, "The Abrasiveness Trap: High-Achieving Men and Women Are Described Differently in Reviews," *Fortune*, August 26, 2014, https://fortune.com/2014/08/26/performance-review-gender-bias/ (archived at https://perma.cc/9WDK-HCXA)

15 Eun-Ju Lee, Clifford Nass, and Scott Brave, "Can Computer-Generated Speech Have Gender? An Experimental Test of Gender Stereotype," *Conference on Human Factors in Computing Systems—Proceedings*, January 2000, doi.org/10.1145/633292.633461

16 Anne Eisenberg, "Mars and Venus, Online," *New York Times*, October 12, 2000, www.nytimes.com/2000/10/12/technology/mars-and-venus-online.html (archived at https://perma.cc/4EFV-ASAB)

17 Marguerite Rigoglioso, "Researchers: How Women Can Succeed in the Workplace," Stanford Graduate School of Business, March 1, 2011, http://stanford.io/1qS7AeG (archived at https://perma.cc/ALZ2-WUKU)

18 Carol Kinsey Goman, "3 Ways Women Can Escape the Imposter Syndrome Trap," TheLadders.com, November 13, 2019, www.theladders.com/career-advice/3-ways-women-can-escape-the-imposter-syndrome-trap (archived at https://perma.cc/433M-6HEN)

19 W. Bleidorn, R. C. Arslan, J. J. Denissen, P. J. Rentfrow, J. E. Gebauer, P. Potter, and S. D. Gosling, "Age and Gender Differences in Self-Esteem: A Cross-Cultural Window," *Journal of Personality and Social Psychology* 111, no. 3 (2016): 396–410, www.ncbi.nlm.nih.gov/pubmed/26692356/ (archived at https://perma.cc/DC4Q-9WLW)

20 Ibid.

21 Woolley and Malone, "Defend Your Research."

22 Goman, "3 Ways Women Can Escape the Imposter Syndrome Trap."

23 Ibid.

24 Carol Kinsey Goman, "Leaders Need Flexible Body Language," commpro, nd, www.commpro.biz/leaders-need-flexible-body-language (archived at https://perma.cc/D82U-MHRV)

25 Carol Kinsey Goman, "How Female Leaders Can Claim Power Through Body Language," *Linkedin: The Learning Blog*, March 10, 2017, https://learning.linkedin.com/blog/learning-tips/how-female-leaders-can-claim-power-through-body-language (archived at https://perma.cc/JKN4-9UU7)

26 Jennifer Vineyard, "Madeleine Albright Says: Learn to Interrupt, But Only If You Know What You're Talking About," *The Cut*, June 22, 2015, www.thecut.com/2015/06/madeleine-albright-best-advice.html (archived at https://perma.cc/WG5B-HU2N)

27 Goman, "How Female Leaders Can Claim Power Through Body Language."

28 Carol Kinsey Goman, "10 Body Language Hacks to Project Leadership Presence on Video," commpro, nd, www.commpro.biz/10-body-language-hacks-to-project-leadership-presence-on-video (archived at https://perma.cc/3WAT-E4TN)

Chapter 10

1 Wikipedia contributors, "Proxemics," *Wikipedia, The Free Encyclopedia,* nd, https://en.wikipedia.org/w/index.php?title=Proxemics&oldid=934770665 (archived at https://perma.cc/3GCR-FDXM)

2 Carol Kinsey Goman, "Communicating Across Cultures," American Management Association, January 24, 2019, www.amanet.org/articles/communicating-across-cultures (archived at https://perma.cc/5PMB-ZTY4)

3 Kendra Cherry, "Understanding Body Language and Facial Expressions," *very well mind*, 2017, www.verywellmind.com/

understand-body-language-and-facial-expressions-4147228
(archived at https://perma.cc/ZFJ7-KPGT)

4 Carol Kinsey Goman, "Reading Body Language at Work: 5
Mistakes You Don't Want to Make," *LinkedIn Pulse*, April 17,
2018, www.linkedin.com/pulse/reading-body-language-work-
5-mistakes-you-dont-want-goman-ph-d- (archived at
https://perma.cc/5NAC-NW8X)

5 Alia Al Theeb, "The Ruler Should Not Have Any Barrier
Which Separates Him from His People, *Gulf News*, August 19,
2011, https://gulfnews.com/uae/the-ruler-should-not-have-any-
barrier-which-separates-him-from-his-people-1.853465
(archived at https://perma.cc/D5V8-H22G)

Conclusion

1 Carol Kinsey Goman, "Managing Change," *The Sideroad*,
2007, www.sideroad.com/Management/managing-change.html
(archived at https://perma.cc/FM4J-NZ4N)

2 Sigal G. Barsdale, (2002) "The Ripple Effect: Emotional
Contagion in Groups," Yale School of Management Working
Paper No. OB-01, July 30, 2001, http://papers.ssrn.com/
abstract=250894 (archived at https://perma.cc/E3DM-H3BV)

3 Carol Kinsey Goman, "3 Crucial Skills for Leading without
Authority," TheLadders.com, June 20, 2018, www.theladders.
com/career-advice/3-crucial-skills-for-leading-without-authority
(archived at https://perma.cc/EG9L-TDYU)

4 Ibid.

5 "Empathy: College Students Don't Have as Much as They
Used To," University of Michigan News, May 27, 2010,
https://news.umich.edu/empathy-college-students-don-t-have-
as-much-as-they-used-to/ (archived at https://perma.cc/
756B-H942)

INDEX

CPSIA information can be obtained
at www.ICGtesting.com
Printed in the USA
JSHW021447281020
9186JS00007B/52